THE GOLF CLUB

A Novel

MARTIN COHEN

VICTORY BELONGS TO THE MOST PERSERVERING
NAPOLEAN

This is a work of fiction. The events and characters herein are imaginary and are not intended to refer to specific places or living persons. The opinions expressed in this manuscript are solely the opinions of the author and do not represent the opinions or thoughts of the publisher. The author has represented and warranted full ownership and /or legal rights to publish all the material in this book

Published in the United States of America
Create Space Publishing

To my lifelong friends: ED & FRAN, MAL & LORI, BROWNIE and SUE. IF THERE IS AN AFTERLIFE WE WILL STILL BE TOGETHER, AND THAT IS WHAT I SINCERELY LOOK FORWARD TO. If it is to be heaven, which I surely am qualified to enter, I hope it is not overcrowded.

Other books written by Martin Cohen

BETS WISHS DOC: A personal biography of Learning Disabled children in a special school.
"2" A REASON TO BE.
EVERY DAY IS SUNDAY
COLD JOURNEY
IMPLANTS
MURDER, AN ALTERNATIVE TO MARRIAGE
THE END OF THE AMERICAN PRESIDENCY
MADAME GOVERNOR: PUBLIC ENEMY
THE BOY FROM THE MONESTARY
THERE WAS ALWAYS ROOM AT MY MOTHERS TABLE
ONE SHOT ONE KILL
THE PRESIDENTS MASK
THE SEARCH FOR THE SPAGHETTI TREE
TEENAGE HOLOCAUST
A MODERN PASSOVER
ANIMALS TO READ ABOUT
THE LAST PRESIDENT

CHAPTER ONE

SWISH! This force of a golf club with its downward and forward momentum is the sound every golfer wishes to hear right before the small white speckled ball is smacked into a rocket trail into the air, arching up traveling far, and settling where the golfer hitting it wishes it to be. Only the best, the professionals can accomplish this seemingly easy feat with the accuracy and distance required to win. The weekend hackers as they are called can hit the ball, yet in many instances it is only a wish and a prayer that the ball will travel to the exact position intended.

Golf clubs, bags, shoes and all other accessories can be purchased cheaply in Wal-Mart, or extremely expensively in sports stores such as Sports Authority. Many hackers believe the more expensive the equipment, the better they will play. Most professionals have their equipment and expenses paid for by sponsors such as Nike. Many communities or golf resorts can cost highly in fees. However there are many public courses where the hacker can play inexpensively.

The Pine Needle Golf Club set near the Sedona Hills Red Rock Golf Club was an exclusive club whose members were in the upper two per-cent of American wealthy. The club house was created to replicate an old Middle Age Castle. The day room rate was $1,500 per night per person. It was over-ridden by service personnel whose job it was to create an atmosphere of affluence not seen by many people. The carpeting on every floor was lush and thick and made to accommodate the colors of drapery, chairs, lounges, and the muted colors of the pastel designs of the domed ceilings. Each room had a king size bed, a voluminous bath with a large whirlpool. The beds were pure feather, and as soft as velour cushion. Bedding was changed completely daily, as each room was rendered an intensive antibacterial cleansing. Every room had a balcony that was adorned with lounge chairs and a filled bar. The outdoor bar was complimented by a mahogany dresser in which another filled bar was available to the resident. Windows were set to overlook portions of the deep lush greenery of the golf course. Due to its placement in the Sedona hills a cool refreshing breeze soothed every person causing the sensation of a private massage therapist.

Once each year, a millionaire's tournament was held for those who had everything in life that money could buy. Five men sat around a table drinking twenty five year old Bell's scotch trading stories. At first they told tales of their gathering of enormous wealth, and how they had no mercy or caring for anyone less fortunate than themselves. They contributed to charities out of the selfishness of obtaining public fame, and reducing contributions to the IRS. Each had secret financial accounts in and out of the country banks and they never discussed the whereabouts of these accounts with one another. There were some-things that needed complete secrecy. Four of the five men had multiple marriages, as the women they married bored them in time as life did itself, which is except for the accumulation of more money. Making money was their mantra, their life's work and it seemed to each of them to be an endless task. It was their six meeting in 2014, and things in their lives had become mundane.

Myron Schwartz, Henry Calico, Donald O'Leary, Francis Domingo, and Charles Attleboro each sipped the costly liquor and listened to the tales of their friends wanting to be able to top the intensity and bravado of the other. Myron had been thinking for a long while what could possibly entice each of them into some sort of contest that did not necessarily deal with the accumulation of funds through clever and at times illegal actions. "Money, money, that's all we ever talk about," Myron said to his friends. "Life is becoming very boring, and we need to do something to elevate our interest. None of us are kids; we have all achieved amazing success in life and vast fortunes. I have an idea that may appeal to each of you. A challenge event that will be accomplished prior to us meeting here next year. Let me explain what is on my mind."

Myron drained the last drop of Scotch from his glass and he leaned forward on the table placing his arms across it as if physically reaching out to each of his friends. "Listen to me; it would seem that each of us have everything we could ever want, money, homes, trophy wives, children, grandchildren, mistresses and properties, just everything. However, there must be something we want that we do not have, or something we would like to do, Ummmm !, maybe create something new, maybe race a speeding car, maybe bungee jump, maybe rob a bank, maybe commit a murder. There just has to be something each of us wants. I suggest a contest. During this next year each of us will choose to do something spectacular. We will meet here again next year, and vote who has done the most spectacular or unusual thing. The winner of the vote will be given $1,000,000.00 from each of the other four to a charity each of us will support. That could be for medical research, a religious organization, or anything we would all agree on."

"Myron, that is a brilliant suggestion," Charles Attleboro age 64, added. "Yes, yes, all of us agree. Each of us needs to find that one single item we do not have, wished to do, or to create before we die. I think Donald who is the eldest, how old are you Donald?" Charles asked sarcastically.

"Fuck you Charles, not old enough to lie down and die. Nope and I know I will come up with the best endeavor of all of you. Donald laughed, "Old?" "Who's old?" Not me either said Francis, and Henry got a cock so big it will never die. None of us are too old to choose some daring event to accomplish, right Henry," "Yeh, I guess, but what in the world is left to do?" Henry asked ordering another drink.

"Nothing, all you need is imagination and a little guts," Myron chipped in. "One year, twelve months 360 days, think my friends, think. Now let's go out and make scuffs in the green carpet." Charles Attleboro could not play as he had a walking cast on his right foot from an injury he obtained falling off a treadmill in his own private gym. His trainer could not react quickly enough to prevent Charles from falling. The trainer was fired immediately, and as yet, Charles had no inclination to replace him.

The remaining four men split up, two to a golf cart. Each cart was equipped with GPS, range finder, heater, and air conditioner. Myron paired with Henry, and Donald with Francis. They played as a foursome, and although each could well afford a professional caddy, none of them would admit they would not play well or do anything wrong on the course. In actuality, none of them were even adequate golfers, but none of them would admit it to anyone else or to each other. The round of a traditional eighteen holes took them about five hours. Each cheated on the score card, not counting balls hit into the woods, or trying more than three attempts on the greens. "How many strokes on that hole?" Donald asked Francis. "Well I think six would do," he responded, although including the first swing, at which he missed the ball on the tee, and the three shots he took from the rough grass to get the ball onto the green, his actual score was nine.

After finishing the eighteen holes, they decided to have a snack before leaving for the airport to fly home. Myron and Henry each had separate corporate aircraft waiting for them on the tarmac of the airport. Donald, Francis and Charles flew first class to their homes.

Although the men knew each other because of business dealings, they lived in different parts of the country, and Myron was flying directly to Europe. He was going to Poland, to the German camp that his grandparents had perished in during the Second World War.

Chapter 2
1942

The drone of the air as it passed through the engines of Myron's jet and the three martinis he had made him drop off into a deep sleep. He had seen many movies and documentaries about the Holocaust and the mass murder of Jewish people by the Nazi's. He often dreamed of them using information he had gained from his parents about those frightful times.

His Grandparents, Bertha and Michael Schwartz had been in the Ghetto, and avoided being "collected" by the Nazi's. They had taken refuge in a barn on a farm hiding in the top stacks of hay. They ate rodents, and managed to get water from the bin used to water the two horses that were kept in the barn. The piles of hay gave them some warmth during the freezing cold of the harsh winter. No one, not even their closest friends knew of their existence. They had no contact with anyone for fear of being found. One cold and moonless night, they heard cars pull up to the barn, and they saw the frightening beams of flashlights searching. They clung to each other tightly trying not to even breath. However, one of the Storm Troopers climbed up the ladder to the loft and shivering both from the cold and insane fright, they were discovered.

Months before, Myron's father and mother had escaped to England. Myron's father pleaded with his grandparents, however, they refused to leave the homeland, and said to Myron's father, "this is our home, and these are our people, we will be fine. You go, be well and we shall meet once again in Israel." Those were the last words his grandfather spoke to Myron's father. It was only four months later that Bertha and Michael Schwartz were subject to the insufferable conditions in the train that ultimately would take them to the camp and their demise.

Myron's father Bernard Schwartz was absorbedly aware of what was happening in Europe with the rise of Hitler and he made plans to get out of Poland with his family and his friends as soon as arrangements could be made to fly to England in a private plane. He met much resistance as the people who had been under severe Russian rule for many years, actually welcomed the approaching Nazi's as an encouraging relief from the Russian atrocities. Many of the people cheered the approaching Nazis as they forced the oppressing Russians out of Poland and took over completely. This

Anschluss as it was later called was to the very end of the Jewish population in Poland, and the beginning of one of the most horrendous periods of time in all of modern history.

The German camps in occupied Poland during World War 11 were built by Germany in the course of the occupation of Poland (1939-1945) both in the areas annexed by Germany and in the territory of General Government created by the Third Reich. A system of various camps of various kinds was established across the entire country, including extermination camps, concentration camps, labor and POW camps.

German occupied Poland was a prison-like territory. It contained 457 camp complexes. Some of the major ones such as Stutthof and Auschwitz consisted of dozens of subsidiary camps scattered over a broad area. The number of sub- camps under Auschwitz 1, Auschwitz II, (Birkemau) and Auschwitz 111(Monowitz) was forty eight (48). Their detailed description is provided by the Auschwitz-Burkina State Museum.

The camp system was one of the fundamental institutions of the Nazi regime, and with the invasion of Poland became the backbone of the German war economy and the state organized terror. It is estimated that some 5 million Polish citizens went through them. The racist policies of the Third Reich against Slaves and "undesirables" filled the labor and concentration camps from the first days of the occupation. The deliberate maltreatment, starvation, overwork, and execution of prisoners amounted to "ethnic cleansing. Between 1941-1942, the concerted effort to destroy the Polish Jews including those of other European nationalities led to the creation of death camps, constructed for the sole purpose of extermination. It was only after the majority of Jews from all Polish Ghettos were annihilated that the gas chambers and crematoria were blown up in a systematic attempt to hide the evidence of the crimes. Auschwitz was turned into a major death camp by expanding its extermination facilities The ovens worked around the clock until November 25, 1944; were blown up by orders of SS chief Heinrich Himmler.

The primary function of death camps was the elimination of Jews from all countries occupied by Germany except the Soviet Union. (Soviet Jews were killed on the spot).

Bernard Schwartz held many secretive meetings with his friends; however, he had little chance of convincing them of what was occurring. He had accumulated funds from his work as a tailor and his wife accumulated funds from her work as an assistant director in the town's hospital. Together and with the funds of a few other families that wished to escape to England they managed to convince a pilot to make a secretive flight with them to England. It was the wisest decision of his life. For it saved the lives of twenty persons.

"We cannot think of those we left behind, we must look only to the future, he said as they entered the two bedroom house that all twenty of them would live until employment could be found. "We shall soon know how fortunate we are to be here," he told his wife who was eight months pregnant with Myron. "This will only be a stopping point for us. We will work hard and do our best to get to America. The American's have entered the War as their president Roosevelt said after the unexpected disaster occurred in Pearl Harbor. The Americans fighting the Japanese will soon be fighting in Europe. They are the only possibility for peace as they must defeat Hitler. And they will. I am certain."

The constant bombing of England especially London where Bernard and his family had finally obtained a one bedroom apartment in the attic of a Pharmacy was clearly not what he wanted for his newborn son and wife. However, given the scarcity of an available place to live, and his need for work, moving to the countryside was not a viable option. Myron was delivered by a mid-wife who happened to be employed by the local church as a cook. She asked Bernard if he and his wife wanted the child baptized. When Bernard explained to her that he was a Jew she told him that he would be better off becoming a Catholic if Hitler succeeded in conquering England. Bernard thanked her for her concern and explained to her as best he could that in England he had no fear of the Nazis and as soon as he could he was going to take his family to America. The mid-wife questioned Bernard how he would manage to do the trip, however, at the time, he had no idea.

Bernard's earnings as a tailor were meager, and his wife needed to stay in the apartment with the newborn child. He had no idea how to arrange for a trip on a ship going to America, and he had no idea how much it would cost. In addition he constantly heard of German submarines sinking ships with all persons on them drowned. The German's never picked up survivors. He searched for fellow Jews and found a small congregation who held religious services in the ruins of a bombed out market. Every Friday evening he would go to the service and mingle with the other Jews who attended. He was careful not to say much about his plans, but he knew that he needed information and he reached out to the Rabbi for advice.

"If in some manner you could learn a trade of a seaman, and obtain a job on a ship, you might be able to get passage instead of paying for it," the Rabbi said. "Learn to be an electrician, a carpenter, or some-other trade. A tailor is not needed on a ship."

Bernard took out many books from the library which was intact and studied the elements of electrical work. He went to the docks and spent as much time as he could mingling with seaman to learn which ships were going to America, and when they were scheduled to leave. As he walked on the pier one evening he began to talk to a seaman who told him that in a few days a ship carrying English made wool products was to leave for America. Bernard asked the seaman where he could manage to speak to someone in charge of hiring the crew for he told him he was an experienced electrician, and would like to get a job on the ship.

"So you are an electrician," the pudgy man sitting behind the metal desk asked Bernard.

"Yes sir, I got my training and experience in my home-land in Poland. I first worked as an apprentice, and then acquired my Masters license. Unfortunately given the conditions in Poland, I do not have any of those papers with me," Bernard lied convincingly.

"You got any idea how dangerous this run can be, what with them subs on the prowl?" the man asked.

"I am well aware of the risks, however, I would like passage for my wife and child in lieu of wages if that can be arranged."

"It can, but I need you to fully understand the great risk. The chances of us not being attacked are very large, but we need to attempt to keep trade going. England is an Island, and when we are not being bombed every day, we survive very well. For God's sake America is a baby when compared to the largess of England. We have history; you only had a revolution and a few internal wars. We are steadfast in our resolve to defeat this German animal. I welcome your courage and hope you are up to the task." The pudgy man pulled out some papers for Bernard to sign which he did glowing inside him-self.

Bernard could not wait to get home and tell his wife Helga of their good fortune. She was not pleased at all.

Helga what is the matter?" he asked confused by her lack of responsiveness.

"Bernard it is too dangerous. The baby will have a very difficult time. What if he gets sick? Where will we live? How do we get passports?" Helga was overwhelmed with worry.

"Helga would you rather be here, with the bombs, and with the possibility that Hitler will conquer this land?" We cannot take that risk which is much greater and more probable to cause us harm, than an ocean voyage to freedom. We will be alright. I have some money saved. Once in America we will immediately seek out a Jewish congregation and ask for help. We will be fine. Now start to pack. We will be leaving England in two days."

The voyage was extremely difficult. Helga was constantly sea-sick, and the baby had developed a fever. The ship had no medical staff; however, the first mate had some experience, and tried as best he could to help.

"Helga, Helga, wake up, we are near the city of New York. Come up with me, take the baby and you will see a very wonderful sight." Together they stood at the rail of the ship as it passed into New York harbor past the statue of liberty.

"Helga, look at the buildings, there was nothing like it either in Poland or in England. Look, look, we will be home here. It will be safe."

With the help of the friendly first mate, Bernard, Helga and the baby slipped past the United States custom officials, and entered the main terminal of the cargo offices. Bernard thanked the mate and with Helga holding his hand and he holding their one small piece of luggage they walked along the streets of lower Manhattan, smelling the foul odor of the Fulton Fish Market which was nearby. Helga protested to Bernard. "If this stink is what America is all about, then we should take the next ship back to England. It will be easier to deal with the bombings than to have to smell this forever."

Bernard walked out into the street and waved his hands for a taxi to stop.

"Where to mister?" the cab driver asked?"

"Take us to the nearest Jewish synagogue," Bernard said hoping he had enough money in his pocket to pay for the ride.

The taxi stopped in front of a red brick building on which a yellow Star of David was painted on the facing of the brick.

"Is this the church you want mister?" the cab driver asked.

Bernard, Helga and the baby walked into the building noticing paintings and photographs on the walls which depicted Biblical stories from the Old Testament.

"Hello, hello, is there anyone here?" Bernard called out.

An old bearded man approached them and asked, "Who are you?"

Bernard told the Rabbi his story, and was pleased when the Rabbi suggested that they remain in the Temple in a back room that had a bed, and one chair and a small radio. Over the next few days, some members of the congregation sat with Bernard who re-told his story to them.

"Wow! That is really some adventure. We did not really know how horrible it was for the Jews in the camps. Many of us were not even aware of the existence of the camps," one member said.

"How could you not know?" Bernard asked. So many people were killed in the streets. Crystal Nacht when the Nazi's really began to herd up Jews like cattle."

Within a few days Bernard found a small apartment on Nassau Street. Both he and Helga were amazed at the hassled crowds of people on the streets. There were signs in every store window that read, "UNCLE SAM NEEDS YOU" with a picture of a patriotic man pointing to the observer. It was an inducement sign for young men to join the military service. However the draft (military assignment) was in effect and millions of young men were notified that they were being assigned to one branch of the military or another. Since Bernard was an illegal member of New York City, there were no government records that could be reviewed to prove his existence.

Bernard worked through -out the war years in a clothing factory. Helga obtained a young woman to watch Myron and she took a job in a factory that made parachutes for the American flyers. Together they had the ability to live comfortably while Myron was growing up to school age. Kindergarten began when a child reached six years of age. Helga took Myron to the local public school to enroll him; however, she had no identification. No Social Security card, no driver's license, no birth certificate. The administrator told her to go to City Hall and obtain some documentation. She could tell them the story that she was a war refugee, and that the administrator told Helga, they would be able to help her. More upsetting was that for the moment, Myron could not be enrolled in the public school.

That Friday evening, Bernard and Helga told the Rabbi of their circumstance, and he responded by informing them that Myron could be enrolled in the Hebrew School that was run by the congregation, and in time he would assist them in getting proper credentials.

Bernard had what is called in Yiddish as "zitz flesh", the need to do something, to move on, to be creative, to change, and he did. He took their savings and rented a small loft where he began to manufacture men's suits. Within two years he was doing quite well, and then an idea originated in his mind. Now that we were at peace with Japan, perhaps he could arrange to have his clothing made there, apparently very inexpensively in terms of labor costs, and import them and re-sell them in the United States.

In the next ten years with Myron who was now sixteen, and his mother, helped Bernard open another store in Brooklyn, and then another in the Bronx. The two retail outlets were some of the first completely discount stores selling men's wearing apparel.

By the time Myron had graduated from New York University with a degree in marketing, "Bernie's Men' Markets were in nine states with twenty three stores. Bernard Schwartz was a very wealthy man. When Bernard died at the age of sixty two he left the entire clothing empire to his son Myron. Helga and Bernard did not have any other children. Thus Myron inherited a fortune. He ran the business very efficiently and became a millionaire from the profits. He surrounded himself with a group of exceptional financial advisors and he opened retail outlets across the country, in England, France, and Italy adding to his massive financial profits.

Myron stood silently at the rusted barbed wire gates of the camp where his grandparents had been killed. The plane ride allowed him to rethink all this history of his family told to him by his mother as he grew up. She passed one year after his father, and he swore to himself that he would never forget them and their toils in life. As he stood in the dirt of the roadway in front of the gate he had visions of creating a monument to the thousands of Jewish souls that had perished during the war. He knew of Korea, and Vietnam, he knew of the Falkland Islands, and of the collapse of the Soviet empire. However, he did not know if anyone had created a monument in Poland to honor those souls lost to God in an inhumane mass murder of almost the entire population of Jews in Poland, and the millions of other Jewish souls that were beaten tortured or burned in the ovens by a mad man running an insane society. He thought and thought about it. Creating this monument would be his answer to the agreement made with his friends at the golf club.

Chapter 3
Irish whiskey

Donald O'Leary was as Irish as Irish can be. He was thin and tall, six feet seven inches. His body was hard and his temper was mean. He was either your best friend or your worst enemy. He saw things as black and white and never in grey. You would either love him, or hate and fear him. He was meticulous in his appearance and in the Irish whiskey he loved. If you would give Donald a Kilbeggan or a Bushmills the whiskey that had a history of 400 years of brewing behind it, he would be your friend, not that he could not afford to purchase as much of these rare Irish whiskey's himself.

Donald O'Leary had a reputation as one of the country's leading criminal defense attorneys. If you killed one person, or held up a gas station, your crime would not be in league with the cases Donald would consider. If however, you were a famous Hollywood icon, or a major political leader, or the head of a foreign government, or a leader of an unpopular movement you would at least draw his attention. He was as ruthless in his beliefs as he was in his heritage.

Donald taught Criminal Law at Harvard Law School. He was a full professor, and his classes were as brutal as was his personality. He had the distinct reputation of asking a question of a student, who might respond with an incorrect or unreasonably thought out response, of having that student remain standing either until the class was over or until the student could respond with a well thought out correct logical answer. Donald did not play favorites, and passing his class was an achievement every law student strived to do. Only a small percentage of students who took Donald's class passed the first time around.

He was not particularly liked by his colleagues; however, his name on the faculty roster was like a gift of gold which was immediately transferred into monetary funds.

Donald's mind was always in quest for his back-round. He spent his first sixteen years in the foster care system having been the child of a woman who left him on the steps of a church one hot summer evening pinning a small note," please take care of my baby Mary O'Leary. The police and social services tried in vain to find Mary, however after a few weeks the search was halted. Boston Massachusetts had hot humid summer days, and Donald's mother gave birth to him on a park bench along the edge of the Charles River.

On the note she pinned onto the baby; to his blanket naming him Donald O'Leary, a name he never sought to change.

Life for him within the orphanage, and then in the foster care system was one horror after another. He was unresponsive to love and caring and he trusted no-one. During his sixteen years he had been placed in fourteen different homes, in all of which he caused havoc rejected other children or the adults. He spent his time alone as much as he could and he read volumes of books on countless subjects. He enjoyed reading of the Dark Ages and the Kings and Queens that reigned during that portion of history. King Henry the Eighth, a complete despot, and the Tudor Christians, the Borgia's, a family of loathsome evil. When he read the historical accounts of these times and the people that lived within the time periods, his adrenaline kicked in and he savored any opportunity to be able to return to the distant past. At the age of sixteen he was completely weary and shattered by the world he was forced to live in. He graduated from a high School one of many he was forced to attend with academic honors. As he walked across the stage he overheard one of the teaching staff say, "there either goes a genius who will contribute to mankind or a youngster who will incarnate evil in its most horrible sense." "Screw you," Donald thought to himself and placed up his middle finger at the teacher under his robe.

Throughout school he never displayed any sense of humor; he kept to himself, and spoke in only literal fashion. He seemed like a super intelligent robot to his classmates.

Given that Harvard was a free ride for him with complete financial aid, he studied with a fury and intensity to be able to graduate in three years, and to gain a scholarship to the law school. His scores on the law boards were some of the highest ever attained by a college graduate, and Harvard, Stanford, and Yale were very eager to have him as a student in their schools. Upon the interview at Yale, Donald sensed a feeling of false promises from the interviewer and he boldly stood up in front of the woman's desk and told her to screw her-self. Then he walked out of the office leaving the woman in amazement at the complete audacity of the young man. He experienced both interesting and boring classes in law school. He often would disagree with a professor which would lead to a harangue from both sides of the podium. His classmates either cheered him on or frightened of a professor's reprisal would listen in amazement at the arguments that prevailed. Donald graduated at the level of "Law

17

Review", but only given Summa Cum Laud, instead of the Phi Beta Kappa he deserved.

Donald often wondered what his heritage might be. He knew he had a most unusual personality. He felt he was a born leader, but to lead what. That was a question for which he had no answer. For the next few years he worked as a clerk for a local appeals court judge. He knew within himself he was much more intelligent than the judge, however, he managed to keep his feelings to himself and restrain himself from making the judge an enemy, thus causing him to be dismissed. He needed the job and the money.

In one case on the Judge's docket the question of "clear and convincing proof" was in question. Late at night he read the opposing councils reasoning to change a case from criminal to civil. The defendant was a small time crook who had been sentenced to twenty years by a judge with a bug up his ass. The guy had possession of a small amount of weed and the judge in order to make a name for himself in political circles, and gain some publicity brought the curtain down on this first time offender. In a criminal case the defendant's guilt must be proven by the prosecution beyond a reasonable doubt. In a civil case the bar is lower and only fifty one per- cent or something akin to more than equality in favor of the defendant would be enough to win the case. Thus a mere preponderance of the evidence would prove the case to be civil and not criminal. The judge that Donald was working for on the appeal left notes suggesting that the case remain in the criminal court although he did think the sentencing was excessive. The defense attorney had made a motion for the judge to consider sending the case to the civil court, and Donald agreed with the motion the attorney entered.

For the first time in the three years, he approached his boss, the judge and began to question the morality of a man, a first time offender spending twenty years of his life in jail for what Donald thought to be only a minor infraction of the law. The judge listened to Donald argue the virtues of the case and slowly but reluctantly changed his mind and ordered the case be retried civilly. In this matter, the preponderance of the evidence would likely support that a criminal act had been committed, but it was of minor importance and that the sentence should be reduced to time served and community service.

Donald did not know that the man who was involved was a capo (lieutenant) in the Borgosa Crime family. After a meeting with the convicted but free man Donald was given a phone number to call. The man placed it into Donald's coat pocket as he and his attorney left the courthouse happy, speaking loudly, and seemingly joyous.

Donald remained very curious about his past, his mother, his father and his family. Rather than go to a professional to seek some answers, he left the position with the judge and decided to query on a web site similar to Ancestry.com. The only initial information he had was his mother's name "Doris" and no entry on his birth certificate of his father. The birth certificate obtained indicated he was born in 1943, although he doubted its authenticity. He continued to attempt to trace through census records, passport applications, drivers licenses, and in formulation somewhat of a family tree. He finally saw the name of an Irish Patriot, one Michael Collins. Collins was an Irish hero considered to be the initial main personality of the Irish Republican Army.

The Irish Republican Army was an Irish military organization. It was descended from the Irish Volunteers, an organization established on November 25 1913 that staged the Easter Rising in April 1916. In 1919, the Irish Republic that had been proclaimed during the Easter Rising was formally established by an elected assembly and the Irish Volunteers were recognized by Dail Eireann as its legitimate army. Thereafter the IRA waged a guerrilla war campaign against British rule in Ireland leading to the War of Independence in 1919-1921.

Michael Collins (October 16 1890-August 22 1922) was an Irish revolutionary leader. He was the Minister for Finance and Director of Intelligence for the IRA. He was also a member of the Irish delegation during the Anglo-Irish treaty negotiations. Subsequently he was both chairman of the Provisional Government and Commander in Chief of the National Army. Collins was shot and killed in August 1922 during the Irish Civil War. He is held in particular esteem with the Irish population regarding him as their movement's founding father, as Americans look towards George Washington. Collins was a womanizer having many female companions. His lifetime coincided with the period of aggressive, mass agitation for woman's rights. The female suffrage movement in Ireland closely aligned with the campaign for independence.

Donald closed his computer realizing that he was a descendent of Michael Collins, and with this realization of his blood line tied to this hero of the past he began somewhat to understand his own personality. Giving the information much thought he decided to see a

Psychiatrist for testing of his own personality traits. He knew he was not an average person, and his quest for knowledge about himself was all consuming.

"Mr. O'Leary," the doctor said holding a thick file of papers in a folder on his lap. "You are one of many little understood persons who are diagnosed with a type of Autism called Asperger syndrome."

"What in the Lord's name is that?" Donald asked. "Is it that I am some sort of nut job?"

"No not at all," the doctor said placing the file on his desk.

"Asperger syndrome (AS) also known as Asperger disorder (AD) or simply Asperger is an autism spectrum disorder (ASD) that is characterized by significant difficulties in social interactions and often by non-verbal communication, alongside restrictive and repetitive behaviors and interests. It differs from other autism spectrum disorders by its relative and preservation of linguistic and cognitive development. In other words people who show symptoms of Asperger can have great intellectual abilities and can be deep thinkers.

One main aspect of clinical interest is marked verbosity. Young children with (AS) have been colloquially called "little professors" and they use language literally. Like many lawyers, Your-self included. They like you, have particular weaknesses in areas of nonliteral language that includes humor, irony, teasing, and sarcasm. They lack an understanding of the intent of humor to share enjoyment with others, but they do not use it in conversation, and often do not "get the point" of it in written language."

"No wonder three wives have left me," Donald said. "I know that I usually do not "give a shit" about other people, not even my employer, or my clients. The law is the law, and that is it. What is the treatment?" Donald asked.

"Basically there is none. We try behavioral management and sometimes it is successful, but not often unless we get a very young child as a patient. There is no magic pill or medical device that can change what you are. There must be some (AS) genes in your family."

Immediately Donald thought of the personality of Michael Collins.

CHAPTER 4
NOT FOR ME

Henry Calico knew he was black. He was always black. He was born black, suffered the segregation in Atlanta Georgia as a black, and he hated it. He often thought of Michael Jackson and the rumors of Jackson trying to look whiter by using dyes and bleaching products to whiten his skin. There were times when Henry thought of the same thing. He was born in 1950 in a segregated community south of the main city of Atlanta Georgia. He had no idea who his father was and his mother worked in the cotton fields to be able to feed Henry and his brother.

Henry Calico, M.D. had a childhood dream of becoming a physician. Growing up in a single family home with dire poverty, poor grades, a horrible temper, and low self -esteem, he was driven by his dream and his mother who had at best a third grade education. She challenged her sons to strive for excellence. Young Henry persevered and became a full professor of neurosurgery, plastic surgery and pediatrics at one of the nation's most prestigious hospitals and medical centers. He remained in this position for twenty five years.

After the meeting at the golf club he returned to Atlanta. His mind wandered as he stood in front of a storefront medical center and he watched as an endless line of persons who were ill stood in line to gain entry.

He was in attendance as a college freshman in 1960 at Kent State University when a large group of students gathered on the central mall as protesters to the war. The protest got out of hand and three students were killed and many injured as State Troopers fired into the crowd. It had a lasting effect on Henry and his thoughts went back to his early childhood in Atlanta and the history of segregation in the United States. He knew he was only accepted to Kent State because of an attempt by the Congress to create admission equality in the Nations Universities. Each school in order to obtain Federal grants had hidden quota systems allowing less qualified black students to enter in place of more qualified white students. The same quota system existed in Graduate Schools, not only for black students but for Jewish students as well.

Henry was a tall thin person, at least six foot seven inches tall. He played basketball for the University and had acquired many friends both black and white. His hair was tight on his head and wiry. Many times he tried to grow the "Afro" to be in style but his hair would not cooperate. He found he had an almost innate ability to retain information in Biology, Physics, and Chemistry. He dressed in common clothing as was the fashion of the times, however, on Sunday when he dressed for Church, he groomed immaculately. Henry was an accomplished debater, quite often in opposition to the liberal views of most of his classmates. He held his positions staunchly and was adamant when his views were challenged.

Racial segregation in Atlanta like much of the South had known many phases after the freeing of the slaves by President Lincoln in 1865. Jim Crow laws were passed in swift succession in the years after the Atlanta Race Riot in 1906. The result was in some cases segregated facilities, with nearly always inferior conditions for black persons, and in many cases it resulted in no facilities at all available to blacks, e.g. all parks were designated whites-only. In 1910, the city council passed an ordinance requiring that restaurants be designated for one race only, hobbling black restaurant owners who had been attracting black and white customers. In the same year, Atlanta's streetcars were segregated, with black patrons required to sit in the rear. If not enough seats were available for whites, those blacks who were seated had to give up their seats to Whites. In 1913 the city created official boundaries for white and black residential areas. And in 1920, the city prohibited black owned salons from serving whites.

Beyond this, blacks were subject to the South's racial protocol whereby, according to the *New Georgia Encyclopedia*

"All blacks were required to pay obeisance to all whites, even those of low social standing. And although they were required to address whites by the title "sir", blacks rarely received the same courtesy them- selves. Because even minor breaches of racial etiquette often resulted in violent reprisals, the region's codes of deference transformed daily life of ritual, where every encounter, exchange, and gesture reinforced black inferiority."

Henry knew his family suffered this discrimination, and he never forgot it. He knew of the landmark U.S. Supreme Court decision *Brown v Board of Education* which helped usher in the Civil rights Movement, racial tension in Atlanta erupted in acts of violence. For on October 12, 1958, eight years after Henry was born, A Reform Jewish

Synagogue was bombed. The "Confederate Underground" claimed responsibility. Many believed that Jews, especially those from the North-East, were advocates of the "Civil Rights Movement."

Now, as a retired American Neurosurgeon, responsible for many deep brain stimulation techniques to treat Parkinson's disease, and a professor, the author of many text books, and the recipient of plentiful rewards, he stood in the city of his birth wondering what he might be able to do. He had traveled all over the world explaining his techniques on various surgeries, and amassed large amounts of money. Henry was a devout Conservative politician in his belief system for the nation and as devout in his religious beliefs as an Seventh –day Adventist.

Henry had established scholarships, and awards for black students, however, he tried his best to include white students as recipients as well. His political and religious views were not always met with respect for he admitted that although he believed that gay persons were entitled to live their lives as they chose to, he was adamantly against gay marriage. He did not believe in evolution even in light of his medical training and expertise for he felt the wonders of the world and the universe, free choice, and man's ability to make decisions based on fact and empirical data could only have been created by a greater being. He expressed largely conservative viewpoints, although he did not support the banning of semi-automatic weapons. He was a very strong believer in the Second Amendment. He was a staunch believer in morality and ethics which he assessed were God given traits, and did not evolvo historically.

As he looked at the faces of the black populace standing in line in the freezing cold of a winter storm, he knew what he needed to do.

Chapter 5
Prestige and Power

Charles Attelboro and his brother Mark were born into a family of incredible wealth and power. Charles father Ethan Attleboro had acquired many patents for the processes and mechanisms to sell soft drinks in clip off cans. Ethan lived in Allston, Massachusetts before the twins were born. Allston is a small area of Boston on the outskirts of the inner city. Ethan's wife had died in childbirth and Ethan was left with the task of raising two newborn babies. He had little money, How however, his mind was replete with ideas of inventions. He was a small framed man, thins and exhibited much energy both in his speech and motor movements. He was always moving, arms, legs, head, when in school in earlier years he yearned to go to a graduate school to become an engineer. However, family finances and the economy made that impossible.

A young black women lived in the same four story walk up apartment house that he did and he chatted with her often when across the street in the laundry. Ethan had some funds from his wife's insurance policy, and he used this money to sustain his family. However, he had ideas that needed development, and he could not create or work in a workshop while taking care of the infants. He asked the woman if she was available for a few hours a day for minimal wages to take care of the children. She agreed, and Ethan rented a small room at the rear of the laundry to become his workshop. He worked with aluminum to create differing types of storage containers. Finally, he designed a can with a flip top cap which could be hermetically sealed. He realized that food and beverages could safely be placed into the can and those products sold to the public instead of buying freezing products or large quarts of beverages.

He sought a patent attorney to help him prepare the papers to submit. Surprisingly the patent for the aluminum can was approved. The attorney had done his work for a percentage of profits if the can was accepted for manufacture and retail sale. Ethan sent letters to many of the top manufacturers of sparkling beverages and was beyond surprise when the Coca-Cola brand notified him that they wished to pursue a face to face meeting, asking him to bring some samples of his aluminum can with the pop top. Years passed and Ethan's fortune grew exponentially. He was rich, and became wealthier and wealthier as time passed. He decided living in Allston in the small apartment was not good for the boys who had been attending a local public school. Both boys were bright, but were denied social growth. Ethan a mild mannered man wearing black horn rimmed glasses rode the "T" to downtown Boston and entered a Real Estate office.

Ethan called Bruce Kent his partner and attorney to meet him at the real estate office to help him make any decisions. Together, they walked into the prestigious offices of Prime Boston Real Estate, located on State Street. Ethan had not ever experienced the glamour and opulence of such settings. He began to feel excited at the complete physical attractiveness of the offices. Compared to his apartment and his work shop in Allston, he felt he had entered a new world. And indeed he had. Ethan being the typical unassuming scientist had absolutely no idea what his net worth was. He left all the financial matters to Bruce. He knew he could write checks for anything he needed, but he did not attend to any particulars. His world was in his workshop. Essentially, he was anti-social and spent time out of the workshop. He had become close to Aretha Williams, the young woman who had taken care of the boys for years. However, his relationship with Aretha was not anything more to him than the fact that she was great with the boys, trustworthy, mindful of his basic needs for food and clothing, yet, no sexual attraction whatsoever.

"Hello Gentleman, welcome to Prime Boston Real Estate, how may I be of service to you," a middle aged woman with flaming red hair, dressed in an evening gown, wearing high heels and moving as if she was a Hollywood movie star. She pointed to her desk. Ethan saw it was polished mahogany wood, and pointed to two plush chairs that she wished them to be seated upon. Soft music played softly in the back-round, at the entire office was replete with fresh flowers. Ethan looked around and could not believe that this was an office.

Bruce Kent began a conversation. "Miss, or is it Mrs. Whittle Baum," Bruce asked looking at the silver plated name plate on the desk.

"It is Mrs. however should you wish you may call me Ivory, my given name. Would you Gentlemen wish to have a drink or some food?"

"No thank you Ivory," Bruce continued. "We are here to find a proper residence in a fine neighborhood for my client Mr. Ethan Attleboro. I represent his interests. He is a famous scientist, now living in his original apartment in Alston, and I think he needs to move to a new neighborhood more in line with his wealth and stature. He has two young children about to enter High school, they are twin boys, extremely well behaved, and they each possess those qualities one would expect of children of such a genius of invention."

"Well I am certainly impressed Mrs. Whittle Baum replied. Can you give me some estimated budget for living quarters?"

Ethan remained silent, allowing Bruce to continue.

"Money is not a consideration for Ethan. I am certain he does not have an inkling of his net worth, however, I do have bank documents with me which will allow you to assess what type of living quarters would fit his financial status."

Mrs. Whittle Baum opened the folder Bruce gave to her and her fair facial skin took on a blush. "My dear Mr. Attleboro, I see that finances will not be a problem for you."

"As I said, Ivory, Ethan is quite a rich man, even though he shows no interest in his worth. What neighborhood would you suggest?"

"Why there is no question in my mind Mrs. Whittle Baum said. I suggest we look at townhouses in the Back Bay, Beacon Hill to be more specific."

"Would you kindly explain to Ethan why you select that area for him?"

"Certainly, first I shall give you some history of the area, she replied."

Beacon Hill was settled in 1625 and its diverse history is traceable and walkable down Charles Street nearly 400 years later. The iconic images of Beacon Hill- the flickering gas lanterns, the red brick sidewalks; the wrought iron fences are synonymous with the City of Boston.

Beacon Hill is a diverse melting pot where generations of immigrants have mixed with the cities elite. Louisburg Square-with its magnificent Greek revival townhouses and private park is the most prestigious address of them all. The Abiel Smith School was the first school for African-American children, and the Vilna synagogue was built to on Beacon Hill to serve the growing Jewish population. The Beacon Hill Preparatory School is still rated quite high in educational acumen.

Beacon Hill and neighboring Back Bay are the elite neighborhoods in Boston.

Today Beacon Hill is regarded as one of the most desirable and expensive neighborhoods in Boston. I would suggest we look at the Beacon Hill Mansion, which is a single family six bedroom, six bathrooms, 7,878 square feet. It has the Boston Public Garden as its front lawn on Beacon Street and it would be a wonderful living space for you and your children Mr. Attleboro. Ethan was lost in his thoughts and was not paying attention to what Mrs. Whittle-Baum was saying. Brian realized that Ethan was lost in his own thoughts and suggested that they get in a cab and proceed to the property that now for sale.

Arriving at the mansion, Bruce was overwhelmed at the rustic beauty of the home, and the greenery surrounding it.

"We need look no further he said glancing at the Frescos painted in the domed central hall ceiling." It was all breathtaking. A complete remodeling had been done in each room and given the massive fortune that Ethan had earned from his inventions and the commissions he obtained from very major manufacturers, and the fact that Bruce felt that assuredly, Ethan would be nominated for a Nobel Prize in Economics, he stated brashly to Ethan that the home be purchased as soon as possible. The asking price for the mansion was 14.7 million dollars which was about the interest Ethan earned in one year on his vast fortune. Bruce prepared the papers and they arranged a closing date.

"Ethan, go home and talk to the boys. They have to be a part of your decision to live here."

Neither Charles or Mark seemed to be enthusiastic about a move. They had grown up in the apartment in Alston and were happy with their friends from the public elementary school. They explained to Ethan that they could find another place to live and remain in Alston with their friends. Neither boy had an inkling of their father's monetary value. He was just the same old father who puttered around across the street in a room behind the laundry. When he was away on " business" Aretha took care of them and saw to their every need.

"Dad, if we move into this new place will Aretha come with us?" Charles asked.

"Not only will she be welcome to be with us,, but her entire family can come as well. Aretha had one young child who was six years old, and another daughter from an earlier marriage who was twenty two.

"Can we go and see the place you are considering?" Mark asked.

"Sure, we will go tomorrow and I will have Bruce meet us there as well. I think you boys will be absolutely thrilled."

The next morning traveling by cab and not the "T", the four of them rode into Beacon Hill.

Aretha was the first to realize what an enormous change in their lives was about to happen. She looked at the exterior of the home and she was amazed at the wealth they represented. The astonishment increased as the cab stopped in front of the mansion and Ethan paid his fare and asked the cab to wait until they came out.

"I gotta keep the meter running sir, " the cabbie said.

"Fine" Ethan replied," and when I return to your cab, estimate what it would cost me to purchase it, and pay you to be my personnel driver. Of course we might need a more modern vehicle, just think about it please."

Mark whispered to Charles as they approached the front door. "Shit!, what the hell is going on here?"

"Got me bro, I have no idea. Maybe pop has lost his mind."

After a tour of the mansion the boys and Aretha were speechless. "Pop, how the hell can we live here? It's gotta be a monster fortune," Mark said walking out the front door completely amazed.

Bruce sat down on the steps and motioned Aretha and the boys to sit with him. He said. "I think it is time for all of you to know that your father who often has his head completely in the clouds is a billionaire. He has made fortunes of money through his inventions and investments. The money he has could support an army of people. He has no idea, nor does he ever seem to care about money. He just dithers away being a creative genius, and you two boys will one day realize just how fortunate you are to be his sons."

Ethan and the boy's, along with Aretha and her son moved into the mansion. Bruce hired decorators and contractors to do any work that needed to be done. Ethan asked for a room for himself in which he could work. "Not a problem sir," and Ethan's basement was finished into a modern laboratory the likes of which he had only seen at trade shows or trade magazines.

He knew he needed to find a nice school for the boy's in which they would get their High School education. He also wanted them to enroll in a Catholic School. Ethan was quite a practicing Catholic, and he never missed a Sunday mass when he was home. When he was away Aretha took the boys to the Roman Catholic Church in Alston on Commonwealth Boulevard.

Cathedral High School was ranked very high in the catalogues Ethan studied. He and the boy's visited the school, and all three felt that the school was a good fit. It was not far from their new home, and the Priests and teachers all seemed to be sincere, warm persons who took education very seriously. In this school the boys would get a fine education to prepare them for excellent colleges, and at the same time Ethan knew their Catholic education would be continued, a factor he was impressed with. He spoke with Father Delgado, the schools headmaster, and he was impressed at just how "regular" a guy he was.

"Father could you tell me how an average day will go for my boys? I know Mark is very interested in athletics, mention the Red Sox, or the Patriots to him and he will immediately give you a litany of statistics."

"He will also increase his knowledge of the Apostles Creed and the Nicene Creed. I am certain you know sir that the Nicene Creed in the authoritative expression of the fundamental belief of the orthodox Catholic Church. It is the recitation we begin each day with.

Ethan responded. "My son Charles seems to be very interested in Catholicism. He learns from my day care person, he watches Catholic programming on television when possible, and he looks forward to Sunday Church services when either I take him or my day care person Aretha takes him. Yet my other son Mark is only interested in sports. I wonder what he will feel about coming to a Catholic school. I do believe he would want to delay a High School education altogether, let alone one combine with religiosity. However father both boys will attend school together, and as far as I am concerned, my choice will be here with you. Let me make an appointment with you to bring the boys in for a tour, and to give them a chance to meet you, and you them."

"I look forward to meeting them," Father Delgado responded shaking Ethan's hand.

After the tour of Cathedral High School, Charles was bounding with energy. He could not stop speaking. Mark on the other hand was fearful of expressing his displeasure with his father's choice however he dared not speak.

"Our sacred text is the Bible, the Old Testament and the New Testament. The books of Scripture firmly, faithfully, and without error teach that truth which God, for the sake of our salvation wished to see confided in the Sacred Scriptures. The mystery of the Most Holy Trinity is the central mystery of the Christian Faith and of Christian life. The Son is consubstantial with the Father, which means that, in the Father and with the Father the Son is one and the same God."

Mark Attelboro held his I-phone under his desk as Sister Ann-Marie continued her elemental dissertation of Catechism. It was one P.M. and the Red Sox were coming to bat in the fifth inning of the American League playoffs. This was of much more interest to Mark and he let the Sister drone on as he watched his small screen with the sound off. On the other hand while Mark sat in the rear of the room, Charles sat in the front row taking copious notes, listening intently.

The four years passed slowly for Mark and not slow enough for Charles. Father Delgado realized that Charles would be attentive to a suggestion that he enter a seminary to train for the priesthood. He knew as far as Catholicism was concerned the brothers were as different as white and black. Mark had been going to a gym after school and his body, even as a teenager was conditioned for sport. Charles on the other hand was quiet and demure constantly studying, and his grades reflected all his work.

Charles sat quietly in front of Father Delgado's desk, Ethan sat beside him.

"Ethan it is my sincerest opinion that Charles should go to Seminary and study to become a priest. I would suggest Saint John's Seminary for its reputation is beyond reproach, and it is here in Boston in the Brighton neighborhood. It is a Catholic major seminary sponsored by the Archdiocese of Boston. It was founded in 1884. The current Rector is Monsignor James P. Morovey. He was able to hold the seminary together even with dropping enrollment when the unfortunate disgusting facts about Catholic Priests committing unmentionable crimes upon children was revealed in the early nineties. In preparation for a Catholic priesthood St. John's offers a four year program leading to the Master of Divinity Degree.

Charles felt his heart beating in his chest. He was sweating not from fear but from enjoyment and pleasant expectation. Ethan was elated when Charles committed to Father Delgado that he would be thrilled to begin his studies at St. John's.

Mark had refused to go to the meeting with his father and his brother. He walked on State Street until he was near the Common's. On the sidewalk was a sign about the United States being in the war in Afghanistan. He knew we had attacked Iraq, and killed Saddam Hussein. He also knew that the President had sent in Navy Seals to eliminate the head of Al-Qaeda, Osama Bin laden, and the person responsible for the Trade Tower terrorist attack in New York. The sign was being held by a woman protesting our involvement in Afghanistan and he bristled. What kind of American could she be? President Bush had eliminated Hussein, and President Obama eliminated Bin laden. However, American's were not safe from terrorism and he felt he had a calling to help protect. Thus, he went to a Navy recruiting station, and being eighteen he did not need his father's permission to enlist.

Ethan was distressed when Mark told him of his decision, but he yielded to Marks desire to serve. Thus both his sons would be in service, however in very different ways. After he spoke to Bruce, he drew up his will leaving all his assets in equal shares to his sons. He was getting old, and when he went to bed at night he awaited for the sunrise, not the sunset. That would come soon enough.

Charles thoroughly enjoyed his education, and he kept in touch with his father and brother by writing copious letters of his learning and experiences. Mark on the other hand was in Afghanistan, a Navy Seal on a covert mission. It was his second deployment. As much as Charles training was mental and philosophical, Mark underwent the most demanding mental and physical conditioning offered by the United States Armed Services.

The average United State Navy Seal spends over a year in a series of formal training environments before being awarded the Special Warfare Operator Rating and the Navy Enlisted classification (NEC) 5326 Combatant Swimmer (SEAL) or in the case of a commissioned naval officer, the designation Naval Special Warfare (SEAL) officer. All Navy SEAL'S must graduate from the 24- week "A" school known as Basic Underwater Demolition, a parachutist course, and the 26 week SEAL Qualification Training Program. Not many initial enrollees make it through. To be a Navy SEAL was to reach the epitome of service in the United States Armed forces.

Charles was in the office of Father Delgado, back at Cathedral High School . Father Delgado had in his hand a letter from Bruce. Ethan had died from a sudden heart attack when he received two

Navy SEALS at his door announcing that Mark had been killed in Afghanistan on a secret mission. Charles could not contain him-self ,and he fell to the floor crying, his body convulsing. As much as he tried to remain at St. John's he could not. His depression prevented him from leaving the mansion and nothing Aretha could say or do, other than provide him with food helped. She and Bruce pled with him to return to his studies however, he felt God for some reason beyond his understanding had a plan for a different life for him. He did not have the inventive mind of his father, nor did he have the physical attributes of his brother.

        Now years after the shattering news, he was pondering Myron's challenge. He had inherited his father's fortune and he needed to do something exceptional. But what?

Chapter 6
Against the Law

Salamanca Spain is one of the richest, highest income, most beautiful areas of Madrid South of Barcelona. If a person were looking for high art, fashion or food, this is the neighborhood in the country of Spain where a person will find the best of the best, including voluminous amounts of illegal drugs, especially cocaine. Calle de Serrano is overflowing with designer labels, designer drugs. Upscale and trendy restaurants on Recoletes are everywhere. Here on every street you will find exquisite windows to look through and menus to whet anyone's appetite.

Salamanca is known for being one of the wealthiest and expensive areas in Madrid, with a high cost of living and or of the highest real estate prices in the city. Serrano Street is listed as the third most expensive streets in Spain.

A significant number of diplomatic missions are set in Salamanca district, such as the Switzerland embassy, at Villaler Street, the French embassy at Villala Street, The United States Embassy at 74 Serrano Street or the Italian Embassy on Juan Bravo Street.

William Correia was helping to unload a hundred packages of unknown merchandise in the Costa del Sol resort. A dockworker had called in sick, and he went to help his men unload. He had risen to the middle levels of the drug dealers, and it was not usual for him to unload. Here scores of yachts and pleasure crafts dock. The packages were carried to the rear of a small truck that afternoon. The packages contained cocaine, high level, which was bound for northern Europe.

In the Barrio Chino in Barcelona, off the popular Rambla, marijuana, and heroin are bought and sold within the sight of uniformed policeman who chat nearby. Similar scenes would take place each day on the streets in Puerto Del Sol and Gran Via sections of central Madrid, as well as in hundreds of other places throughout the country- evidence that Spain in overrun and overwhelmed by illegal drugs.

The police and other officials said, the Iberian Peninsula had become the prime transshipment point for the European narcotics market, with about half the rugs entering Europe now coming through Spain. Drug trafficking and consumption, along with crime and all the other attendant problems, were the worst in years and becoming worse. Arrests and drug fighting were also on the rise. The Government labeled all this "the Eye of a Storm, and William Correia wanted to get out of Spain with his wife, he could be either arrested or killed by his bosses or the police during a raid. The police were negligent, however every so often they conducted raids. William was not particularly liked by his men for he was a slave master to them. He did not allow for any variances in procedures, and if a man strayed or stole merchandise, he was found in a ditch, a bullet in his head.

The newspaper said that the police had confiscated more than 4,000 kilos of cocaine and believed that represented only about 10 to 15% of the drugs coming in. The paper indicated that drug crackdowns in the United States and Latin America forced traffickers to other markets. The proximity to northern Africa and the Middle East-producers of hashish and heroin respectively made the European market a most viable trade center. Criminal sentences in Spain for possession of 20 kilos of cocaine could result in a three to five year imprisonment, while in the United States it could bring in a twenty year sentence. However, William and his wife Dorothea discussed the situation and decided that they must get to the United States. William felt it was only a matter of time before something very bad would happen to him, and he wanted out, not an easy thing to accomplish.

When William was called to the docks a few weeks later he managed to hide five kilos of cocaine under his shirt and sell it on the street. Together with the immense amount of money he had stashed away, that would give him and Dorothea more than enough money to buy passage on a cruise liner to the United States. He knew that if he was caught, a bullet would enter his skull, and his body would lie in the street unidentified, and rotting until some policeman would call the mortuary and have him sent to be cremated as a vagrant. He quickly disappeared from the dock, returned home, and told Dorothea what he had done. He had the money in his pocket and rather than be seen carrying baggage, he and Dorothea, strolled down the street, took a trolley car to the cruise terminal, bought tickets, and hid in a janitor's closet until they heard an announcement that the ship was boarding. William knew he still had more than enough money to purchase some clothing for them, and he worried about the fact that he had no passport.

The ship was destined to disembark at the port of Miami Florida. William knew he would have to pass through United State customs, and he needed some identification if not passports for himself and for his wife. One balmy evening, around the late dinner hour, William began to stroll down the halls of every deck to see if any passengers had left a cabin door open. His stateroom was on deck two. As he walked slowly down deck four, he saw just what he needed. There was a cabin door slightly ajar. He looked down both ends of the corridor and saw no one. He entered the room cautiously and there in plain sight on a dressing table were two passports. He quickly placed them into his pocket and got onto the elevator. Even though the other passengers on the elevator did not know him, he began to sweat because of anxiety. He got off on deck eleven where he met his wife and he motioned to her not to go into the buffet but rather to come with him.

Together they walked out onto the open deck. The movement of the ship caused a slight breeze and enabled William to compose himself, and he reached into his jacket pocket withdrawing the two stolen passports. My dear Dorothea, we will now be known as Eduardo Domingo and Marianna Domingo. Saying this he showed her the stolen passports.

"Where did you get these?" Dorothea asked looking at the two documents.

Lying, William said, on the floor in one of the corridors. With these we will not have any problems with customs. I also have been thinking that we should not disembark in the United States, but continue on this ship which is headed for Puerto Valera Mexico. The Mexican authorities are not anywhere as strict as those in the United States. We can remain in Mexico for some time and then we can go to wherever you wish in the United States. William gave the ships photographer $200.00 to take extra pictures of him-self and Dorothea. He told him he wanted prints of 5"x8"; 4"x6" and small passport size pictures to keep in his wallet. William obtained the prints and got some glue from the ship's general store. Carefully, he pasted the new pictures over the ones currently in the passports. He gave the porter who took their small bags of luggage though the Mexican customs without any problems, and the customs official only took the briefest look at the doctored passports.

After some time, Eduardo and Marianna Domingo left to live in Mexico City. Eduardo was bored and wanted to work. He also became acutely aware of the illegal drug cartels that operated thorough Mexico. From street talk he heard of the Columbian Cali cartel and the Medellin Cartel who were both dedicated to fight with each other for regional control and against the Mexican government. Hundreds if not thousands of Mexicans were being killed. Each cartel wanted control of the trafficking route to the United States.

Columbian Don Marina Mendes was apparently the main exporter of cocaine and had the power to deal with organized crime networks all over the world. Eduardo thought of how he might fit into the scenario since Mexico had long been a major source of heroin and cannabis with drug traffickers already having established an infrastructure that supported the routes into the United States. He needed to find out just who to contact and what side he might be on.

He decided to join the Medellin Cartel and within a few years he was designated to design new routes for trafficking. The United States was becoming more interested in toppling the cartels, however Eduardo foresaw a day in the future when the major cartels would be diminished or destroyed by the Mexican Army, and the trafficking routes into the United States becoming more restricted.

To his surprise and happiness, Marianna announced one evening that she was pregnant. Even though they still possessed the American passports Eduardo had stolen on the ship, they decided that they wanted their baby to be born in the United States and that was enough reason for Eduardo to once again disappear. He had amassed a fortune of money, most of it was cash. Getting into the United States with so much cash presented a problem. He thus went into an international bank and created an offshore account in Switzerland with the cash being transferred to this numbered account.

Francis Domingo, Eduardo's son was educated in a private exclusive school in Westchester County in upper New York State. He was a very handsome boy with dark black hair, almost no facial hair, eyebrows that seemed to be black ink, and an athletic body. He was a rare and extremely talented athlete. His grades in High School were quite good and he graduated with a 3.88 scholastic average. He had played soccer, football, and ran track, setting a new High School record for the 880 yard run. He decided to remain in New York State and wished to attend Union College, a Catholic institution. Although exposed to Catholic tradition and religion, Francis was not at all interested in the clergy or what it represented. He was a fierce competitor and could not grasp the concepts of religion. Francis could not tell his parents of his disbelief, since his only interest was in making money. He majored in business and earned a Master's degree in Business administration. Eduardo provided Francis with more money than Francis actually needed, and he used the excess money to make loans to students who needed money and were willing to sign high interest notes in order to obtain it.

"What do you want to do with your life?" his father asked.

"I am not certain, however, I would like to become a banker," Francis replied.

"What do you know about Banking?" Eduardo asked knowing full well that his son was brilliant in matters of money and investing.

"What would you think if I purchased a bank for you Francis?"

"Do you have a group of investors who would couple and become partners with you?" Francis asked.

"No my son, I tell you that I have enough wealth to achieve for you your dream. We do not need partners."

"You really have the funds to do that father?"

"Yes, I do. I will purchase a small local bank for you and let us see what you are capable of doing."

"My God, where did you ever accumulate that amount of money? We are talking about a few million dollars at least," Francis said lighting up a cigarette.

"Someday I will tell you of my past; however, this is not the right time. Let us begin to research the availability of a bank. We need one I assume that is not in the best financial state, and who's Board of Directors would be amenable to a direct sale, Eduardo said also lighting up a cigarette blowing the smoke up to the ceiling.

A small local bank in Florida was purchased and within the next ten years, Francis had turned it into an international banking institution with major investments, Francis learned about arbitrage, the purchase of commodities in one market for immediate resale in another more profitable market. He created a Hedge-fund which could take long and short time positions, use arbitrage, buy and sell undervalued securities, in differing markets in order to profit from the price differences. He was about ready to go public with it when he received a call from Eduardo that his mother Marianna had been diagnosed with colon cancer, and that the outlook for her survival was at best very limited. For one of the few times in his life Francis cried to his father." Why is God so cruel? We have led decent lives. We have tried to help our people as much as we can. You must take mother to the best Oncologists in the world."

"My son, it is too late. Your mother cannot be helped. She has little time left. Come home to say goodbye."

Sitting in the living room of Eduardo's home in Westchester were his lawyer and Francis best friend from college, Donald O'Leary a lawyer whose fame was beginning to be well known throughout the country. O'Leary, Francis knew had close ties to the Borgosa crime family in New York, and O'Leary's reputation grew as he succeeded and prospered in obtaining favorable decisions for members of the Borgosa family in criminal court.

Eduardo sat in deep thought. He came to the conclusion that his son would be inheriting his massive fortune upon Eduardo's death, and he decided to allow his attorney to tell Eduardo where the fortune had come from. Francis listened intently as the attorney sketched out the involvement in the Spanish drug money, the illegal passports, the involvement with the Mexican Cartels, and the immigration to the United States. "Your father is amazingly rich, and he needed for you to know where all the money he amassed came from. When he passes it will be yours, as he had changed his will from sharing with your mother who unfortunately is now deceased to leaving all of it to you upon his death.

"It is time for you to know what is going to be in my will Francis. I know that you have become wonderfully successful and that your future is going to be amazement to the entire world. You have told me that your liquid assets are in the hundreds of millions of dollars and when I pass you will become a billionaire. I have in certain offshore accounts massive amounts of money earned I must admit in not the most legal of ways. I am leaving all this to you when I pass. Mr. Reynolds my friend and my attorney will give to you all the information you will need to do whatever you wish to do with my fortune. By adding to your own, I believe you will be listed as one of the richest men in the world, a fact that will indeed be true.

Eduardo died from a massive heart attack some months after the discussion with Francis. In the evening, sitting on the balcony of his Florida estate, looking at the moonlit streaks passing over the crest of each wave, Francis felt lonely and tried to ferret out his thoughts. He wanted a family, children, a wife, not just the many servants he had that waited on him hand and foot. He had few friends and his five Florida banks no longer excited him. He became deeply depressed and cruel to his staff. He had no pastimes for enjoyment. Dinner was eaten every evening alone in his home. Even in college he did not entertain the thoughts of girls or sex. He had no time for those frivolities. The evening of his senior prom he was earnestly on his computer purchasing stock from an overseas company that had been invested in a spring toy device for children. The stock had dropped in value considerably and doing massive research Francis saw the future of the device, and felt it would become a Christmas favorite and that the value of the stock would rise. He was correct as "Slinky" became and remained a child's favorite.

In attempt to break his state of depression and taking the advice of his Psychiatrist Francis decided to take lessons in golf. He was still athletic and he began to play. He joined a luxurious golf club in Westchester New York, and had Donald O'Leary as his partner. Their friendship grew and as they played Donald told Francis of the many criminals, especially those in the Borgosa family that he had defended.

Donald O'Leary had been married twice, and divorced twice. He needed, he suggested the warmth of a woman's body as much as possible. He was not interested in having a family, only sex. Donald realized that Francis was not interested in Donald's sexual conquests, and wondered if in fact Francis was still a virgin, or in fact if Francis was gay. He knew that if he approached the subject with Francis it would be a delicate conversation, but his curiosity led him to broach the subject one Sunday afternoon on the golf course.

As they were driving to the ninth hole, Donald said. "Hey Francis, tonight I have a date with a hooker, very high class, comes from an agency that I have dealt with for a long time, why don't I call them and arrange one for you as well. These girls are great, good looking, bodies you could die for, and they are prepared and willing to please you in any manner you wish."

Francis did not reply immediately, and Donald pressed the issue. "We can take them to the club for dancing, dinner and rent a couple of rooms and have some fun. It's all on me"

"I don't know Donald. I think I need to be on my lap top to close a deal in China tonight."

"Don't be a prick Francis. Let one of your associates close. The Chinese won't care as long as they get the money, and while they are smiling so will you."

As they finished playing, Francis agreed to the evening of drink and fun. He did so reluctantly being ashamed of his virginity and lack of any experience. Mostly, he did not want Donald to know all this.

Together they walked into the club and Donald immediately went over to the club manager. Francis could see that Donald was negotiating, and at the same time he knew well that whatever Donald wanted he got.

"We are all set my friend. We got two rooms, here is your key. Dinner at 7:00 and the girls will meet us at the bar at 6:30."

"How will we know who they are?" A naïve Francis asked.

"Shit you ass hole, they will find us. Two really good-looking guys sitting alone at the bar. C'mon you do not have to be a genius to understand that these girls are pro's. Haven't you ever called "Rent a Girl? Donald asked draining his first drink"

Not wanting to reveal his insecurity, Francis drained his drink and responded by telling Donald, "Yeh sure, but not here at the club where so many people know us."

"O.K. upstairs to shower and change. Let's get our street clothing from the lockers and begin a night of pure ecstasy," Donald replied signing the bar bill.

At 6:15 that evening, both Donald and Francis met at the bar and ordered drinks. At almost 6:30, exactly, two young beautiful woman walked over to the bar and asked," Donald O'Leary; Mr. Francis Domingo, we are Susan and Laticia, "the woman was wearing a green low cut dress revealing ample cleavage. Laticia was a brown skinned woman who clearly looked Latino. She immediately took the empty seat next to Francis and in Spanish asked, ¿Estás listo para un señor maravillosa noche?" (are you ready for a wonderful evening sir?)The two couples were shown to an empty table set off to the side of the room in a corner, partly excluded from the harangue of the rest of the noise and loud music.

Francis blushed slightly and shook his head in an affirmative. "Please give the ladies drinks," Donald ordered.

All four walked down the hallway, and Donald bid Francis and Laticia goodnight as he placed his room key into the electronic lock and entered his room.

Francis did the same and both he and Laticia entered his room.

"Would you like a drink from the in room bar Francis asked."

"No, not really but I will go to the bathroom," Latica said closing the door to the bathroom. Francis removed his jacket and sat on the edge of the bed full of anxiety. His legs swung in dystonic motions as he thought of just what would next happen. The door to the bathroom opened, and Laticia emerged completely naked displaying the body of a magazine model, completely shaven, and her dark hair falling in cascades to her shoulders. Francis drew in his breath, as his chest heaved from the pounding of his heart.

"What would you like to do," Laticia asked smiling moving closer to him.

"I have to make a confession to you," Francis said. I don't know if you know that I am a very wealthy man. I have spent all, and I do mean all of my time making money. I inherited vast amounts of money from my father, however, during my life I have not had any experience with woman. None."

Laticia moved closer to Francis and bent down on her knees and began to unbuckle his belt. "I assure you that you will always remember this night," she said. "I need you to relax, and let me take you into the universe of sexual pleasure. You friend Donald has paid for my services, and he has absolutely no idea, I don't think of your virginity. I am proud and happy to be your teacher. Now stand up and take off your clothing."

Now some thirty years later, Francis was in deep thought about Myron's proposal.

He opened his morning paper as he sipped on the herbal tea.

"Fifteen Year old student kills four at South Carolina Campus."

He read the story and as he did he remembered the Boston Marathon, the killing at Fort Knox, the children and teachers killed in Connecticut, the 9/11 massacre, the recent incident at Purdue University, the killing in the movie theater, and other murderous killings by most likely deranged youngsters and adults. In all the circumstances, the killer committed suicide. He thought deeply of the incident wherein a young girl of fourteen committed suicide by jumping off a tall tower after being constantly bullied by classmates. He read on and then closed the paper and came to a scenario as to what he could do to help. If he could figure out a plan, he would be able to present it to Myron and the others at the next meeting of the golf club.

Chapter 7
A Dream of Reality

Myron Schwartz had a plan to create an unforgettable, magnificent, tribute to his family and his heritage. He got on his private plane and asked the pilots to file a flight plan for Warsaw Poland, the Capital City of the Country. He wanted to meet with both the President Bronislaw Komarowski, and the Prime Minister Donald Tusk. Prior to speaking with them he needed to gain knowledge of the Holocaust that his grandfather and grandmother had been victims of and of which his father had the foresight to escape to England and live. He took with him historical books to read on the long trip. He read:

The Holocaust was a genocide official sanctioned by the Third Reich during World War 11. It took the lives and executed of three million Jews destroying an entire civilization. Only a small percentage survived or managed to escape beyond the realm of the Nazis. The Holocaust in German occupied Poland involved the implementation of German policy of systematic and mostly successful destruction and atrocities against the Polish Jewish population. The official Nazi explanation for the exterminations of the Jews during their occupation of Poland was the euphemistic phase, "The Final Solution of the Jewish Question. Every arm of the sophisticated German bureaucracy was involved in the killing. German's companies bid for contracts to build the crematories in concentration camps run by the Nazis.

Throughout the occupation, many Poles-at great risk them-selves and their families engaged in rescuing Jews from the Nazis. Gaged by nationality the Poles represent the biggest number of people who rescued Jews during the Holocaust. However, no any reported the existence of the death camps in their country.

Prior to World War 11 there were 3,500,000 Jews living in Poland about 10% of the population. At the end of the war over 80% of Polish Jewry perished Treblinka extermination camp located 50 miles northeast of Warsaw, the capital city of Poland saw 1,200,000 Jews exterminated. Auschwitz located about 50 miles west of Krakow was fitted with the first gas chambers where about one million Jews from across Europe were exterminated. Over 30,000 Poles were executed for helping Jews by hiding them, or supporting the Jews living in the wild with food and water, and guns.[1]

Myron had been to Israel and visited the Yad Vashem memorial museum where Polish people who helped Jews during World War 11, a large number of them post humously, the "Polish Righteous" award.

He found out that during the occupation a large amount of official anti- Semitism was encouraged by the Catholic Church and some political parties, but not directly by the Polish Government in exile. In

---

[1] Wikipedia Encyclopedia

fact he was surprised to learn that it was the polish Government in exile that identified the extermination camps to the United Nations.

He felt it strange to learn that at first the State of Israel was refused allowance to have its own exhibition in the Museum of History of Polish Jews since it was in Warsaw and since the Jews of Warsaw were no citizens of Israel. It changed in 1960. This is all for a people who had lived in Poland for over one thousand years.

Myron had arranged a combined meeting with the Polish Prime Minister who was the head of the government, Mr. Donald Trusk, and the President who was the head of state, Mr. Bronilaw Konarowski. With them he visited Auschwitz the German concentration and extermination camp. It was now a large tourist site and set up somewhat as a museum. Auschwitz was the most notorious symbol of the holocaust and Nazi cruelty in the world. It is located in the town of Oswiecim near Krakow. These territories were all occupied by the Nazis during the war.

They returned to Warsaw and Myron was pleasantly surprised. The President, Mr. Trusk told him that Jewish life is thriving in Poland today. He said in a recent visit by Israeli Prime Minister Benjamin Netanyahu, he found a Jewish community virtually unrecognizable to any student of history. That's because, Mr. Trusk continued, after the fall of communism and more than seventy years after the Nazis annihilated three million Polish Jews (of the 6 million total Jews murdered),Polish Jews are embracing their identity and faith in inspiring and unbelievable ways.

He continued, "And that is not just because there is a laudable Museum of the History of the Polish Jews which opened in 2013 or a moving tribute to the anniversary of the Warsaw Ghetto. It was an uprising in the Ghetto during the war that brought special attention to the bravery of the Ghetto fighters so many years after their heroic actions, it's because the countries 26,000 Jews- though a far cry from the millions that built a robust Jewish civilization throughout the pre-war Poland-are eager to innovate Jewish life through street festivals, educational and religious programs, and by investigating their families past, despite the pain.

"May I add something to this conversation?" Myron asked.

"Certainly" Mr. Trusk said.

"In my country a few years ago movie director Steven Spielberg created an iconic film entitled "Schindler's List, the brutal Nazi Amon Goeth proudly hails that he and his soldiers are about to destroy 600 years of Jewish history in Krakow. And although they succeeded in liquidating the city's ghetto and sending the survivors to the death camps, the winds of history have apparently shifted to prove him wrong."

Myron continued." I feel that from what I have learned and seen, today in song and prayer, and even in terms of new forms of Jewish self-expression, Jewish life in Poland is blossoming. And that is cause for celebration and I wish to help extend this new birth. I wish to purchase twenty five square miles around the periphery of the Auschwitz camp to build a new modern town which I will call "Shalom Village," " a Village of Peace" "In Hebrew Shalom means peace. A venue in which not only Jews will live, work, pray, and flourish as well as continuing to contribute to mankind."

It took two months of meetings with the Polish legislature, the unions, and a special mandate published all over the country to have Polish people vote on the acceptance or rejection of Myron's dream. The building of Shalom Village would provide jobs for hundreds of skilled workers, and all salaries, costs of materials, medical care would be paid by the "Shalom Village Foundation" a foundation, created and funded entirely by Myron. Myron would purchase hundreds of World War 11 Quonset huts in which the hundreds of workers could live for the five years to complete that the construction might take He invited Israeli Prime Minister Benjamin Netanyahu, the President of the United Nations, and the Pope as well as leaders of the Polish Jewry and legislature to come to the groundbreaking ceremony. All attended.

Myron hired the largest advertising and marketing agency in the United States to provide methodology for acquiring modern pioneers from all over the world to come to live and work in the new community. The only requirement for the5,000 initial residents were that they were good people, having to undergo intense psychological examination to prove they were prejudice free. All would be taken care of. If a Jew or Jewish family wanted to live or work in the new town, Myron would give them $100,000.00 tax free money to begin their new lives, with the signing of a mutual contract requiring that person or family to commit to five years of residence. He imagined that it might be difficult to have Jewish people live in a village surrounding the horror of Auschwitz. It was his assumption that in time the proximity to mankind's most horrific terror, desensitization would occur, and that new generations of Jewish people would not forget the horror, but to relieve their consciousness of it. If the contract were broken, a portion of the start-up money needed to be returned to the foundation. Non -Jews would also be given the $100,000 dollars as well. Advertising information ran on television all over the world. All social media had similar advertising. The ad simply stated that a new community was to be built and inhabited by interfaith pioneers. Myron did not want to create another Jewish Ghetto, however, he hoped that "Shalom Village" would become a monument to man's ability to be loving and understanding, free from prejudice and hatred and he felt strongly that was how human beings should be. The site of the former Auschwitz camp must be a constant reminder to the residents of "Shalom Village", that peace and good-will must be in the minds of man. Iran, Iraq, Syria, Egypt, so much of the Middle East was at war. A large portion the Mideast unrest was sectarian. The town would have at least;

Homes
Retail Stores
Banks
Medical Care in the most modern hospitals
Mail service
Utilities (free)
Amusements including theaters, live theater, and monuments from a animatronic Moses coming down with the ten commandments, to a replica of Noah's ark
Synagogues for all Jewish sects
All types of places of worship
And every amenity any modern town could possibly have.

The marketing agency had persons from every walk of life answer the ads. It was would their job to accept enough differing people with all varying back-rounds, business persons, teachers, doctors, athletes, retailers, writers, Rabbis, Priests, Ministers, and a cacophony of humanity. Most towns or villages are formulated and developed by virtue of more natural conditions, e.g. climate, sea access, natural resources, etc. Shalom Village was a man- made composite of modern religious life. It was Myron's deepest dream to have success of his experiment, and the winning of the Golf Club contest.

Chapter 8
A Reversal of Fortune

"What the hell happened?" Donald O'Leary asked of the man sitting opposite his teak desk, sunken in the velour chair which was resting on thick white carpeting in Donald's large ornate office on the 57th floor of the office building in lower Manhattan New York City. Muted sounds of the traffic below seeped through the double paned glass windows that reached from the heavily carpeted floor to the ceiling. Standing in front of one of the windows gave a person the feeling of being in mid-air. It was not a place of comfort for any person who had any fear of heights.

" Shit! Mr. O'Leary Vincent Comenico responded, she was a high priced hooker and she went completely nuts. I opened the door to my room and saw immediately that she was stoned. For Christ's sake the room was filled with the odor of the weed she was smoking. The detectives found bottles of Oxy, Percocet, and small packages of something called Vitality which must be some synthetic drug sold legally in convenience stores especially the Seven-Eleven's. Those geeks from Pakistan will sell anything they can make to get people high and there are no laws preventing them from selling it. I mean it she was completely nuts. I came in and began to scream at her. She went to the dresser drawer and pulled out the nine millimeter I keep there, you know, in case, well she grabbed it and pointed it at me while she was screaming. I grabbed for the gun, it went off and I got hit here in my shoulder. I swung at her and smacked her hard on the side of her face. Then she ran to the window and just jumped out. The cops asked me to go downtown with them and they put me in this room. I know the first thing I do is ask for my attorney, you, and I do not say anything. The fucking nut job committed suicide. The cops are just looking for some reason to pin it on me, saying that I threw her out of the window because she pissed me off. Not true, I mean it , not true."

"Great story Vincent, but is it believable. I mean who jumps out of a window because of an argument. Most suicides are mentally disturbed people in deep depression. This was a high class girl, she had to have plenty of money, and what kind of depression could she have been in. Sure she was an addict, but all they want is more drugs. Not a reason to fly out the window. If she needed more drugs you would have gotten it for her, right?"

"Yeh, no problem. But I got a past, you know I was inside for five years on a burglary rap, and then another for beating the shit out of some guy who was behind on payments. Borgosa don't take no for an answer. Someone don't pay, or is late and he ends up hurt. First time we take it easy, then if ever again, well you know.

"Well Vincent, you are a lucky man because Mr. Borgosa has retained me to defend you if any charges are brought up. We will have to prove reasonable doubt to a jury to get you off. I want you to think of anything that might point to your involvement other than the argument with a drug addict who apparently was out of her mind. We know they will find your DNA, we know her body or clothing will have your DNA,... "Wait a minute counselor, she was stark naked, she didn't have no clothing on when she decides she was a bird and she could fly. The cops ain't going to find nothing.

"Vincent you know anything you tell is completely private. You have to trust me. Think real hard, is there anything you left out?"

"No Mr. O'Leary, that's it. You got the story."

"All-right Vincent I want you to find another place to live or go to a friend's home. The police forensic team is searching your old room to find anything they can give to the police as evidence. If they find anything, the D.A. gets it and a subpoena will be issued for your arrest and arraignment. If they find any evidence that the D.A. finds compelling, you will be charged, most likely with second degree murder. Stay low, if the police want you they will come to me to find out where you are. The D.A. will question you prior to the charges. If for any reason this goes to trial I will be there with you, and do not forget, I will be with any time the police want to speak to you, anytime, anywhere. So go and let me know where you are."

Donald sat back in his leather lounge chair not thinking for a moment that in a rage after being shot that Vincent did not render the girl unconscious and then just throw her out of the window. These were the type of sociopaths that he often had to defend for Borgosa. It made him very rich and very famous. He needed to wait until the forensic team of the N.Y.P.D. finished their examination of the apartment. He was ready to prepare a motion to eliminate all of Vincent's past criminal history from a jury if in fact the judge decided to hold Vincent over for trial. If any evidence was found at all, Donald was certain at best it would be circumstantial.

Circumstantial evidence is indirect evidence. It tends to prove circumstances surrounding the fact in dispute rather than the fact itself. Once these circumstances surrounding the disputed fact are established, the jury may infer that the disputed fact did occur. If the relationship between the fact and the circumstance is too tenuous, the circumstantial evidence will not be admitted at trial. It must be closely related to the issue involved in order to have value as proof.

The forensic team prepared the girl's body for transit to the morgue for the Medical Examiner to conduct an autopsy in order to clearly determine a cause of death. Another team went into the apartment wearing coverings on their shoes, gauze head coverings, and surgical gloves. It was their job to attempt to discover any evidence that would indicate what had happened in the apartment that evening. A written report of their findings and that of the medical examiner were presented to the Judge for determination if there was any or enough evidence, direct or circumstantial that a crime had been committed, or if as Vincent reported in his statement that there was an argument and the girl crazed on drugs jumped out of the window.

The team took fingerprints from all of the objects in the room. On the floor they found the nine millimeter gun the woman used to shoot Vincent as he had claimed. They placed the gun into a cellulose evidence bag to give to a ballistics team. They finger printed the window sill and also underneath the window sash. DNA samples were taken in the bathroom, the bed, the window, the pillows, the blanket and all clothing that was in the closet and in the dresser drawers.

Forensic science is a methodology of gathering and examining information about past or present events. It is used in law enforcement where forensic science is used in relation to a criminal law. And it is used as a form of legal evidence. Donald began to think of a motion to present to the judge in case Vincent was to be held over until trial. Vincent was out on $250,000.00 bail. Donald's thoughts were based on a triad of legal premises, "no witnesses, no leads, and no problem." The facts of Vincent's past criminal back-round might tip the scale of reasonable doubt in this case that would be presented by the D.A.. Donald felt strongly that Vincent's legal rights would be violated if his past history was presented at trial. He sought a directed verdict, no jury however that was entirely up to the judge. It was extremely important to Donald that Vincent's past be inadmissible. He should be judged only on the incident that occurred in the hotel room that eventful night. He had no witnesses to present at the present time, however, his research assistant was directed to go to the hotel and find out if any guests that night, near, next to, underneath, or above the room Vincent was occupying heard or saw anything. Should there be persons of interest and if the judge held the case for trial each witness would be asked to respond to questioning in a deposition. This would be a series of questions, presented by Donald as the defense attorney, and in opposition by the District Attorney. Getting the motion approved was of intense value to Donald.

As Donald was writing the motion for Vincent, his secretary rang and told Donald that Pablo Estavo, one of Borgosa's personal assistant's was on the line sounding in a state of urgency.

"Hello Pablo, what's up?" Donald asked trying to continue typing on the key board of his computer.

"The boss needs you to get down to the 108th Precinct in Forest Hills Queens. Seems one of the drivers ran a red light on Queens Boulevard and got into a heated tussle with the cop. The cop cuffed him and pushed him into the patrol car. No doubt we think it was a set up. The boss thinks that the Feds were onto the truck and set up a false traffic situation so as to be able to examine the contents of the truck. You know what was being brought in. It was headed for the Verrazano Bridge into the club on Staten Island. We need you to get the driver out, NOW!."

I'll get my driver and head out at once. Vincent's case can wait.

Donald walked into the 108th precinct and was greeted by the desk sergeant.

"What can we do for you counselor?" the police sergeant asked.

"I am here representing Fernando Domingo, a truck driver recently stopped for running a red light on Queens Boulevard. I do not understand why he was placed under arrest for running a light and not just given a traffic violation."

"Well, as we booked him counselor, the police report on the scene was just given to me and it states that he assaulted an officer, and under piles of lettuce he had in the truck was fifty or so kilos of cocaine. Thus he is in the slammer."

"I need to speak to him," Donald said giving the sergeant his brief case to examine as he walked through the metal detector.

Donald walked down the hall way replete with the odor of stale urine. It was something he had gotten used to over his years as a defense attorney.

Fernando Domingo was in a cell with no other prisoners. The guard opened the door allowing Donald entrance, closing it with a heavy metallic resounding smash.

"Who are you?" Fernando asked of the man in the silk suit, shiny patent leather shoes, carrying an engraved leather briefcase.

"I am your attorney, from Mr. Borgosa's office. Tell me what happened."

"I was hauling my load up Queens Boulevard when I heard the siren and saw the cop car behind me signaling for me to turn off, into the Macy's parking lot which I did. This female cop gets out of her car and comes to my window asking for my license and the truck registration. I tell her the truck is a rental and I have been driving up from Mexico. I reach to get the paper from the glove compartment when she pulls out her piece and tells me to make sure she can see my hands. I ain't got no complaint with her, so's I get the paper, and she goes back to her car to run the plates and registration. She comes back and tells me to get out of the tuck and open the back door. I say's this is a refrigerated truck and if I open it, the produce will spoil. She jabs me in the gut with her piece and slams me into the truck. She forces me to open the door, and then cuffs me to the door handle. Then three suits come out form another car and they go into the back of the truck. They throw the lettuce all over the place and they find the stuff. I tell them I did not know that anything but the lettuce was in the truck. I do not examine my cargo, I just drive. Then one of the three suits uncuffs me, places my hands behind my back and forces me into the other car and they take me to this shit hole.

I asked to be able to make a call, and no-one listened to me. They just threw me into this cell. How did you know I was here?"

"Every vehicle that is in the fleet that Mr. Borgosa uses is equipped with GPS technology, and the techs saw that the truck was stopped, and then headed to a different destination. They became suspicious, and traced the truck and found out within minutes that it was headed for the police garage."

"No shit, they can tell where the drivers are all the time?" Fernando asked surprised.

"Did the cop give you your Miranda rights, you know, you have a right to an attorney, anything you say can be used against you in a court of law, etc.?"

"Nope, no one said nothing to me. She just pulled out the piece and here I am. I only told her that I was a delivery driver, and I don't know what I carry in the truck. Look at my nose. I am bleeding from that pussy slamming me into the truck for no reason. Police brutality counselor that is what it was. She had no right to slam me.

"Alright Fernando, you speak to no one, only me. I will be in touch with you very soon to get you out of here."

Donald arranged Fernando's bail and had him released pending an indictment hearing before a Grand Jury. He knew that the Grand Jury is the sole venue of the District Attorney and that the accused can have no defense attorney present at the proceeding. Donald decided to give this case to one of his staff until and or if the Grand Jury found cause for guilt and the Judge ordered a trial date. He felt Vincent's case, of murder was more important and that he alone would work upon it. He was also distressed from the workload Borgosa pressed him to work on. He had enough money for a lifetime of luxury, and he started to think of ways to divest himself from the long dangerous arm of Borgosa. There had to be a way out of that man's control of his life. "I am getting older and it's time for me to give all this up." He decided to face Borgosa himself and he booked a flight to Mexico City.

Emanuel Borgosa lived in one of the boroughs of Mexico city. Donald took a private cab for the drive to Alvaro Obregon in the north –central western area of the city. Mexico City is composed of neighborhoods which have been no jurisdictional autonomy or representation. Alvar Obregon is one of the wealthiest boroughs It is modern, artistic, and prosperous. Emanuel Borgosa built a large sixteen room ten bathroom, 22,000 square foot home in the hills. The house was surrounded by flat land with no vegetation except for grass. A large high electric fence surrounded the entire property. Security cameras were located completely around the compound and multiple video screens were watched twenty four hours every day by teams of security experts. Small airborne drones reconnoitered the grounds to aid in the establishment of an impenetrable fortress.

Arriving at the entry gate, Donald got out of the car and swept a card into a receiver slot which had been given to him by Emanuel. He heard the growling of the Doberman's who were in cages with electronic door releases that opened upon the gate keepers command to attack any intruder. Donald had not ever before been to Emanuel Borgosa's home. The estate's grounds were immaculately clean, the grass trimmed like a carpet.

Although he knew he was an invited guest, his adrenaline kept pumping into his body making his heart race and pound. The guard, who was fully armed, walked him up a pathway that led to the house. Step where I step the guard said, that is if you do not want to step on an exploding device. Never in his life had Donald imagined such security. But then, Emanuel Borgosa was not an ordinary man. He controlled a large portion of the worldwide drug trade and had control of many of the Mexican cartels. He cared little if they fought each other for supremacy, no matter which one temporarily rose to the top, he always got his share.

Entering through the large, massive marble door which slid on some lubricated track Donald was in awe of the center hall. Donald was rich, very rich how-ever he could not imagine the environment he was now in. The man servant took Donald's coat and ushered him into a room paneled in marble slates from the floor to the ceiling. A massive glass and crystal chandelier hung from what appeared to be a pure silver chain from the beams that crossed the ceiling. He was directed to sit on a leather chair in front of a fireplace in which a roaring fire made flames that danced and swirled in demonic fashion.

"Donald, good afternoon, I hope you are comfortable." The deep robust bass toned voice was emitted from behind him and once again his heart pounded. It was Emanuel Borgosa himself.

"Oh, yes, Mr. Borgosa, I am quite comfortable, thank you," Donald said standing up to shake the hand of his benefactor and superior.

"Would you like something to drink, whiskey, fine wine, tequila, anything at all?" Borgosa asked sitting down opposite Donald.

"Uh, no sir, thank you for asking, however, I am not allowed to drink any type of alcohol. You are aware I am sure that only six months ago, I had some surgery on my heart, some bypasses, and some stents. The cardiologist told me no alcohol ,no cigarettes, no nothing,"

"Not even the company of a lovely woman, Donald?"

"Well there are exceptions, but I am very careful not to exert myself much at this point."

"What is it that I can do for you other than to extend to you my personal thanks for all that you have done for me over these years?"

"Well sir, I think I must stop my employment as a defense attorney. I do not think I am physically well enough to continue the high pressure of the job and I do not want to let you down. For example, right before I left to come to speak to you there were two new cases, Vincent Comenico, who might be charged with murder because of the fact that a woman he was with went out of a hotel window, and the case of the truck driver Fernando Domingo. I felt I had to turn over the Comenico case to one of my staff, it can go either way for him and I was personally going to defend the truck driver which I feel is going to only be a case of minor assault and resisting arrest by an overanxious female police officer. There is no evidence, nor can the prosecutor find any evidence that Fernando knew of his cargo. He will claim he just hooked his van to the carrier and headed towards his destination. Apparently in the officer's haste she hit him into the truck, did not read him his Miranda rights, nor did she make out a proper police incident report. It is my belief, that he may get a month or two in jail but that would be it.

"Donald, you do not have to worry about Vincent. I recently got word shortly after you got on your plane that he had an unfortunate accident crossing New York's fifth avenue. A hit and run as they say. He is no longer your client or mine, he is dead. I hear he was an incompetent druggie, and if he was placed on trial he might say too much."

Donald gulped as silently as he could. He had come to personally ask Emanuel Borgosa to release him from serving as the main defense attorney for the Eastern Region which included Maine to Florida. Donald was frightened beyond imagination as he tried to maintain his composure, and bring up the subject of his need to retire to this master criminal who was no doubt a socio-path.

"Mr. Borgosa, my trip to see you personally, involves my wish to retire from the active practice of defense law. I am not well, and to tell you the absolute truth, I am tired. I have had my fill. Knowing how god you have been to me over the years, I felt it would be a personal insult to you if I did not come to you to ask you to enable me to retire," Donald said waiting with great apprehension for Borgsa's reply.

"Donald, all through the years you have done very well for me. I respect you and thank you for everything. I imagine all things must come to an end and in preparation for this very moment, I can tell you we have engaged another firm to continue your good work. You will receive a lifetime pension from me, and you will never be closed out of my home or my heart. I need you though to finish the case of Vincent Domingo. He is a good man, a family, and he works very hard for us. We need him to be free. Will you do this one last case for me Donald?"

Feeling very relieved, Donald leaned forward in his chair and shook Borgosa's hand, and in return the master drug lord got off his chair and kissed Donald on both of his cheeks.

Returning to his office Donald had two thoughts to ponder. One was to present the case for Vincent, and the other was how to win Myron's challenge. All his professional life he dealt with some of the lowest scum, hardened criminals, all out to do no good, and now he felt deep within his soul it was his time to do something good.

The trial was soon to come and Donald met frequently with Fernando to prepare him for any cross examination if in fact he decided it was necessary to put Fernando on the witness stand. He knew that Fernando was a weak man, and would buckle under the intense questioning of the prosecuting attorney. To do so, Fernando might reveal facts about the continuous shipment of illegal drugs into the United States by the Cartels which in time would lead directly to the house of Emanuel Borgosa. This could not be allowed to happen.

Donald pondered. Miranda rights arguments was a he said she said case, and he doubted if the jury would take the side of Fernando against a policeperson. The police woman's assault on Fernando was a minor issue against her claim that Fernando was resisting arrest.

Donald needed to first prove that Fernando was not culpable because what he was being accused of might be wrongful conduct but not criminal. He might be charged with smuggling illegal substances, bringing goods into the country which is prohibited. Federal law prohibits the importation of illegal drugs, those that have not been prescribed by a physician. There are many penalties for smuggling, including seizure of the items, a search and seizure of vehicles and such. The police therefore upon suspicion could claim they had the right to open the truck. But what if the driver was an old man, white, and non-threatening? did the police then have any right for a search and seizure? Donald thought not and made entries into his log to argue that the search and seizure was against Fernando's civil rights as he was an American citizen. A civil rights argument would completely throw the prosecutor off guard. The more Donald thought about this line of defense the more credible it became to him. The Fourth Amendment to the Constitution prohibits the unreasonable search and seizure of a person or his property. The Fifth Amendment provides that "no person shall be deprived of life, liberty, or property without due process of law", and the error in not providing Fernando with Miranda, in Donald's mind would exclude the argument of he said she said. The police are required in the 14th Amendment to observe due process before interfering with a person's right to life, liberty and property. The arresting officer did not observe the due process regulations and thus could not should not have assaulted Fernando, or search his truck without probable cause. She had no reason to confront him except for speeding.

On the day of the trial after all depositions had been taken, the prosecutor after being told by the judge that his case was weak, decided to offer Fernando community service and drop all charges connected with the illegal transport of illegal drugs into the United State. The prosecuting attorney could not offer sustentative evidence for the errors of the police. Clearly everyone knew that Fernando was most likely a drug trucker for the Mexican Cartels, but there was no legal evidence to prove it. It stood that Fernando was an unknowing carrier of the drugs, and was horribly treated by the police. He was set free, and Donald's career as a criminal defense attorney for the Borgosa criminal empire was over. Now he had to attend to Myron's challenge.

Chapter 9
Differences

Ethel Schwartz was busy at the kitchen counter preparing dinner for her-self and for Myron. Their two children Robert, age 23, and Elizabeth 26, had long moved out of the house to be on their own. Robert had graduated from Stanford and was working for a Pharmacy preparations laboratory after taking a major in chemistry. His sister Elizabeth was working in a large retail department store, which Myron thought was a waste of her talents and intelligence. She had graduated from New York University with a Masters in Advertising. She told her parents she needed experience in retail so that she could become more sensitive to trends and management before she applied for a job at any major advertising agency. Myron and Elizabeth had an argumentative relationship since she was a teenager.

Ethel Schwartz and Myron were married for forty one years and their lives were compatible and quite comfortable with Myron's successes. Money was never an issue and they took great joy in traveling the world prior to Elizabeth's birth. Although they were "holiday" Jews, attending Synagogue services only on the High Holidays, Ethel did light the Sabbath candles and both her children attended Hebrew School to prepare for their Bat and Bar Mitzvoh's. Elizabeth could see no reason for her attending or having the ceremony when she turned thirteen, but Ethel insisted, while Myron took a back seat.

Ethel wanted both children to attend private elementary and High Schools. Once again Myron remained very passive and told her to do what-ever she felt was best for the children. It was rare that Myron and Ethel argued. He was totally consummated with expanding the business and making money. He did take a one month vacation every year, and while initially only Myron and Ethel traveled alone, once Elizabeth was born and later Robert, these yearly vacations were planned by Ethel to include the children. Myron had suggested to Ethel that their next family trip should take place in Israel. Ethel felt it was much too dangerous in that portion of the Middle East and she was reluctant to agree. However she assented and they made plans to hire a private jet and take close members of the family with them, all on Myron's dime.

Many people who visit Israel experience a deep insightful religious experience. Until Israel became an independent country freeing itself form the over-seer, England, being a Jew was only belonging to a religious sect, thousands of years old. Jewish was not a nationality, and Jews had the nationality of the particular country they were born or lived in. Once Israel became an independent country, being a Jew, was a nationality with a homeland. You could be an "Israeli", or a Jew in any country of the world. On May 14, 1948, David Ben-Gurion read the Zionist prepared Declaration of Independence and Israel became a nation. It was said to be an unbearable day, with a hot desert wind blowing across the land from the East, much like a blow dryer. After thousands of years of persecution, the Jews now had a homeland, and they fought Arab and Palestinians in major wars to keep their homeland and the main city of Jerusalem as its Capital.

Myron, Ethel, and Robert and Elizabeth walked up Benyahuda Plaza gazing into all the store windows, very much aware of all the Israeli soldiers that were all about. Myron felt insecure, but acknowledged Ethel's internalization of the culture, and archeology of the ancient land. It took a lot of convincing to get both Robert and Elizabeth to join Myron and Ethel on this trip. Both were aware of Myron's new project in Poland, and Elizabeth unsympathetically objected to Myron's dream of this village built to be built around the Auschwitz camp. She felt deeply in that it was rubbing coarse salt into the wounds of those who had feelings, lost family members, or those who wished it had never occurred, and she included those who secretly held deeply within their consciousness continued hatred, and wished the camps were still functional.

Although Elizabeth and Myron did not live in close proximity to one another, Myron and Ethel had set firmly in the minds of their children that a Sunday phone call to speak to one another was set in stone. Both parents wanted to learn of their children's week, their health, and any new relationships. Ethel was more demanding than Myron, but she was insistent in her demand since the children first left home to be on their own. This led to weekly arguments between Elizabeth and Myron about his project in Poland. She openly expressed her anger and deeply held conviction that Myron was in over his head with the project, and that in time those who bore extreme hatred and loathing would stand in his way, overtly or covertly. She worried for his safety.

The foursome continued their walk alongside the shops with Robert constantly holding his cell phone to his ear. He remained a few steps behind his parents and sister, Elizabeth strained to hear his conversation because she was certain he was speaking to his friend, a young man he worked with, who like Robert was gay. This was a fact not known by his parents, but something he had discussed with his older sister, feeling she would be more understanding and he knew she was extremely liberal in her view of life. He also knew his parents were rigid They were Conservative Republican's and he feared if he came out to them, he would be disowned by his father, even though Myron gave all appearances of being understanding of the differences in life. More than Elizabeth, Robert could not understand his father's building and funding a village of peace in an environment that connoted only fear, hatred, and death. It was a puzzle to him, and something unlike his sister he would not entertain any discussion about it with Myron. The concept and building of this village in Poland was so against the personality of a demanding, strict, exacting personality Robert had known his father to be that he was perplexed by the change in his father's personality.

A portion of their tour was to stop and see the Jewish memorial to the Holocaust at Yad Voshem. They walked into a dark, chilly, solemn environment behind a long line of visitors. In front of them they saw photographs, re-creations of the horrible cells, devices, bunks, and the actual ovens retrieved from Auschwitz in which members of viewing families had met with the horror of being burnt alive. Television screens were muted with stories of survivors, and Robert felt sick and ran out of the museum to get fresh air. He walked around the rear of a large rock formation and vomited the entire contents of his stomach. His mind raced with thoughts of his father's foolish attempt to build a village around the past horror. He also wondered if any of the Polish people collaborated with the Nazi's during the holocaust. Certainly in the modern era, not many or any of these early Nazi collaborators were alive. Yet thoughts and feelings, as well as believes tended to run through family lines and he did not doubt that there were many children and grandchildren who were taught from early ages to hate. Wasn't this true of the "skinheads" in the United States.? Wasn't it true at Waco? Wasn't it true at Kent State?

Elizabeth, Myron and Ethel walked solely with the stunned crowd not speaking. Tears rolled down Ethel's face and she sobbed silently into her hander-chief not being able to grasp the reality of what had taken place at this time of horror. Myron was resolute in his thoughts that Shalom Village might be a modern living symbol that humans could live in peace. The entire mid-east was exploding with war, and devicivnes. Leaders were being expelled by public outcry. Politics, religious animosity, and madness driven by the quest for power were being exhibited in Egypt, Libya, Ethiopia, Ukraine, and many other nations. Iran was threatening the world with nuclear power, and Yemen seemed to be the central heartbeat of the Al-Qaeda organization with cells all over the world. The United States had spent billions of dollars in the wars within Iraq, and Afghanistan not to mention the lives of American soldiers. The Pakistan Prime Minister ordered air strikes against Taliban camps on the Afghan borders. Bashar Al Assad, the Syrian dictator was bombing and killing many of his own people to remain in power. Myron wondered if this combined with the robust and extremes in weather conditions all over the world were not the Armageddon the bible spoke of. Currently the area of the greatest military battles was in the mid-east, the geographical region of the birth of the Judean-Christian beginnings, and the regions of the generation of both the Old and New Testaments. The Book of Revelations reveals the coming of Armageddon, the sites of gathering armies for a battle during the "end times", which could either be interpreted as either literal or symbolic. If it all began in the middle-east, would all of it end there? This was the question Myron was fighting with in his own mind. He felt strongly that Shalom Village would be the one place on earth at which Armageddon would not come. Peaceful and harmonious living would protect mankind. The village could be a new Garden of Eden.

Chapter 10
Harm's Way

"We have fought the Russians, The French and the United States. What did they win? They all gave up and led us to the freedom we will soon have over our own countries. We need to make another worldwide statement like September 11 was in the United States. The battles in our own country, in Yemen, in Pakistan, in Iraq, in Libya, in Afghanistan and in Egypt will be over in time. We need to make an international statement one that will show the world we are solidified, even though our own agenda's might be somewhat different. It is time for all Muslims to exert efforts to bring the infidel to his knees. The Muslim brotherhood must unite. Al-Qaida, the Talban, and all other sects must unite, and create the most comprehensive Jihadist organization all over the world. We need an international target to strike to demonstrate our proficiency and capability to strike at the heart of the infidel." Abu Khalid al Swaheri was speaking. He was designated as the First Minster of defense for the newly combined terrorist forces.

Sitting quietly at the end of the conference table was Yussaf Yaddalah, a well know international terrorist who had a few years prior blown up a large cruise ship in the middle of the Ocean. A resilient Midwestern sheriff, one Sean Carmichael was his arch enemy and almost caught him in the midst of the desert when he, Yussaf blew up a car burning an old American Indian woman to death without the slightest concern. In the confusion of the law enforcement forces that massed at the scene he was able to escape, walking over twenty miles across the arid, scorching sand until he reached a town where he boarded a train. With false passports to utilize in his escape he finally returned to his beloved land of Saudi Arabia.

Also seated at the table were, Ayman al Zawahiri, the mastermind of bombs. To his credit went the underwear bomb, the sneaker bomb and the bomb planted in the printer cartridge of a computer. Fortunately all were discovered and those persons who had the bombs on airplanes were apprehended and were now in highest security jails. Zawahiri was still being sought by the American government for fear of his genius creating a new undetectable device.

Mallah Ahaiddullah the Afghanistany Deputy Minister of Foreign affairs, and Ovar Ahmadullah, the Minister of Intelligence, sat in silence until Ovar Ahmadullah spoke.

" A few months ago, perhaps five or six, an American multi-billionaire began a project in Poland surrounding the old Nazi concentration camp of Auschwitz. He calls it "Shalom Village", a village of peace where it is his dream to create a town of persons living in complete harmony and peace, undisturbed by the violence of the rest of the world. This Myron Schwartz is a dreamer, and we have intelligence that they are still seeking skilled workers worldwide. Actual construction is underway I believe we should implant enough of our skilled workers we need men who are willing to die for the cause. We must plan carefully, and when ready, strike. To demolish a village of peace will no doubt make a world- wide statement."

Zawahiri waved his hand to an attendant. "Bring in the machine," he said walking to the far end of the room. The attendant wheeled in a table on which where a computer and a printer.

"What is so special that you take up our precious time with these common objects? Yaddalah asked.

"Nothing special at all, however I am going to demonstrate to you how we shall achieve our goals without anyone ever being able to detect how we did what we can do until we take complete and absolute responsibility. Now watch carefully."

"This is an ordinary 3-D printer.. It can make any object on demand. A growing array of 3-D printers has already begun to revolutionize the business of making things in the real world. Anything from the smallest part of a watch to the portions of a car. In the United States molds of human parts are being made as frameworks to be covered with stem cells, becoming living tissue as transplant organs. They have successfully produced human ears, fingers, and the President has given billions of dollars to companies that will render parts to the military as situations call for them."

He continued turning on the computer and the printer.

"3-D printers work by following a computers digital instruction to "print" an object using materials such as plastic, ceramics, and metal. The printing process involves building up an object one layer at a time until it is complete. A person can design an object on their computer using 3-D modeling software, hook the computer up to a 3-D printer and with the 3-D printer, and build the object right before their eyes. I am going to make a boot, a belt buckle, and a pair of suspenders. The material I will use will be C-4 explosive. Let us see what will happen."

All the men gathered around the computer table and watched Zawahiri form a three dimensional boot for a left foot. Within minutes the printer replicated the boot, then the belt buckles, and then the pair of suspenders. They did not see Zawahiri build into each item an explosive trigger mechanism that could be activated by a 3-D formed device in the belt buckle, or by a remote cell phone.

"Lets us go outside and ask for a man who is not afraid to die for Allah."

A line of men sixteen in all stood shoulder to shoulder on the desiccated sand. Zawahiri pointed to one man and told him to put on the boot, the belt, and the suspenders. Zawahiri took his hand and placed it upon the belt buckle. "When I raise my hand you will press the belt buckle against your body as hard as you can." The man nodded his head in understanding. "Now walk at least fifty paces from us and watch me."

Silently everyone kept their eyes on Zawahiri. Slowly he raised his hand. Suddenly there was a gigantic explosion. All covered their eyes. When opened, the man was gone and a fireball was all that was left.

"Very impressive my brother," Yaddalah said. Yet we need men with assurance they will carry out the task, men who will die for Allah. Saying this he withdrew his pistol and walked down the line of the fifteen remaining men and suddenly shot five of them in the head.

"These men were not ready to die for Allah. For the rest of them preparations for their 72 virgins are now being made."

Chapter 11
Pills

Dr. Henry Calico traveled around the decimated area of Atlanta where he was born to a single mother and went to school with only black students, many of whom were either on drugs, beginning to form gangs, and who little or no respect for the neighborhood. They played basketball on a concrete surface using a fruit basket as the hoop. Crude skate boards were made by stealing the wheels off roller skates and nailing them to the underside of boards taken from the fruit stands on which fruit much of it rotting had been placed for sale.

Actual hand guns at this time in the early sixties were not as plentiful or easy to obtain as now in Henry's time frame of the present. Instead, the wooden corners of the fruit boxes were the guns with tight rubber-bands nailed to the underside, drawn around the top corner, with pieces of sharp linoleum slid under the rubber-bands and when released, propelled the linoleum fragment at rapid speed towards a target, most likely one with whom the assailant was having an argument. It was a time long after prohibition, and the gangs of Al Capone, were long dismembered. The drug trade was now open to black buyers and sellers, and hoards of mostly young students who were purchasers. The drug trade was most prevalent around the MARTA region and in SW Atlanta where the crime rate was 80% per 1,000 persons.

Henry had made an appointment with the members of the City Council in an attempt to purchase land and property in the neighborhood. He was well aware of Atlanta Medical Center which had recently gotten permission from the Georgia Department of Community Health which issued it a licensing permit to consolidate with South Fulton Medical Center making the combination the Second largest Hospital in Georgia. Its new name is Atlanta Medical Center-South Campus , the South Campus portion being the Fulton facility. It is an acute care facility with 762 beds,580 physicians on its medical staff,3,000 employees, and handles more than 21,000.00 inpatient admissions and 162,000 outpatient visits each year including emergency room 24 hour services. It offers level 1 trauma care, stroke treatment, women's services, medical imaging, orthopedics, a sleep center, pulmonary and cardiac care and bariatric surgery. As a private for profit hospital it is owned by Tenet Healthcare Corporation. With all this Henry wondered why it offered no re-hab services in terms of alcohol and drug addiction, and no social services to unwed mothers who represented nationwide,73% of single unwed mothers with children most likely not to succeed. The white population of unwed mothers was reported to be 29%. Henry concluded that this breakdown in family structure was directly responsible for the gangs, the crime rates, the murders, and the lack of employment in his old neighborhood. You cannot get a job without an education or a skill. You certainly cannot get a job sitting on the steps of an apartment house smoking marijuana, or pushing a needle full of heroin into your veins to escape from the real world. Most of the folks in his old neighborhood of SW Atlanta were a culture of entitlement people who handed down from generation to generation the ability to live off entitlement programs. He deeply felt he needed to do something to stop the decay. The decay to him was the lack of social services, and proper medical care for the poor. Atlanta Medical Center although large with a surprisingly good rating after many ill- chosen frauds, was a distance from the SW region and offered mostly acute care in all of is hospitals, did not offer rehabilitation departments or treatments for addictions in drugs, alcohol, family planning, nor did it offer free contraception. He had researched the Hospitals records and found as a specialty hospital it had many previous severe problems.

In 2002 the company was investigated in a kickback scheme and the company became entangled in scandals, as one of the Tenet Healthcare hospitals came under scrutiny for its surgical practices.

In the early 1990s, the company was accused of fraud by admitting thousands of psychiatric patients who did not need hospitalization, and then charging these patients inflated prices. In 1991 the federal government investigated the company for fraud and conspiracy. In 1993 the offices of the company were raided by law enforcement in an attempt to show that the company was defrauding patients and insurance companies. In 1994 the company paid $2.5 million to settle lawsuits from 23 patients at its psychiatric hospitals. Again in 1994 the company settled fraud charges with the United States involving payments of $380 million USD at the time and federal guilty pleas on eight criminal counts by two of its units.

In the late 1990s through the early 2000s a Tenet owned hospital was investigated for carrying out unnecessary heart surgeries on over 600 patients. Tenet agreed to pay a $54 million USD fine to the federal government and the state of California without admitting wrongdoing. The settlement did not preclude civil or criminal charges against individuals of the company. In order for the company to continue receiving Medicare, the company was compelled by federal regulators to sell the unit. It did; to a subsidiary. The company subsequently paid an additional $395 million USD to 769 patients to settle litigation for unnecessary surgeries.

In 2006, Tenet agreed to pay $725 million in cash and give up $175 million of Medicare payments, for a total of$900 USD in fees to resolve claims it defrauded the federal government for overbilling Medicare claims. The company sold 11 hospitals to finance the settlement. Now after all that financial the company agreed to enter a five year corporate integrity agreement with the U.S. Department of Health and Human Services. That agreement expired on September 2011.

In 2006, a doctor and two nurses who worked for a Tenet Hospital in the aftermath of Hurricane Katrina were taken from their home late at night in highly publicized arrest on charges of second degree murder in the deaths of two patients by the Louisiana Attorney General. In August of 2007 a New Orleans grand jury declined to indict the three women. A New Orleans judge expunged the women's arrest. Tenet once again planned to sell the Medical Center, no one knew the purchaser was an unknown foreign subsidiary, that had purchased all the Tenet sold properties in the past.

In 2011 a Public Campaign committee criticized Tenet Healthcare for spending $3.43 million on lobbying and not paying any taxes in the 2008-2010 periods, and instead getting $48 million in tax rebates, despite making a profit of $415 million, and increasing executive pay by 19% to $24 million in 2010 for its top executives.

Henry finished his recorded testimony before the City Council by saying, "Gentleman, there is an old proverb, Once a Thief, Always a Thief. As of the 2010 perversion of profits making by Tenet, the company who now runs and administers the Atlanta Hospital, have not been investigated. However, that is your problem. The SW District is mine. It is crime laden, with little to no medical treatment, no walk-in clinics, and no rehabilitation programs. It is a complete crime ridden welfare society in your City, and nothing to date has been done to alleviate its specific problems. I am a very wealthy man, and I feel deeply that I wish to attempt to improve conditions there. I ask for permits to;

1. Construct two medium size hospitals with complete community services as non-profits.
2. Construct four non-profit walk in street medical clinics with emergency room capacity, including proper staffing, X-ray ,and MRA capabilities, and small surgical suites.
3. Have three EMR mobile units in the community, keeping one of the three on a rotating basis on the streets.
4. Hire 50 post war veterans, and train them to act as a non-violent community patrol to stave off gang activity, with the power to arrest.
5. Open all accounting books to any members of the council or appointees, to be available for inspection at any time.

Within two months Henry got all his permits and the process got underway. He forgot the bet with the members of the Golf club and worked day and night to get his projects completed. Two large warehouses were torn down and reconstruction for the hospitals had begun. Four deserted and boarded up retail stores were in the process of being converted into the walk-in clinics. Henry placed want ads in all the local and state major newspapers for construction workers, nurse practitioners, Physicians Assistants, secretaries, medical record specialists, Psychologists, Social Workers, Adoption Assistants, two attorney's, Physicians, Dentists, Nurses, and for men who he would have trained as his street patrol personnel. The response to his ads was overwhelming. Almost immediately he had to set up an office complex just to screen applications and interview prospective employees. He had never been happier in his life. He felt that within a five year period of time the hospital and clinics would be self -supporting. He wrote with the aid of his Chief Attorney, Michael Brinkley, and a document contract that each employee needed to sign. It indicted that each facility would take as payment for services any and all insurance payments, to anything from some payment to completely free services to those in need. Patients would not receive not be responsible for payment. Henry was prepared to cover all costs until the facilities could operate without his financial assistance.

Henry hired a public relations firm to continually store information about the soon to be medical services to the community. He was interviewed by local news television and radio stations, the newscaster in all were wary of any hidden intentions on his part. He said clearly, there were none.

With the results of recent surveys, Henry learned that about 44% of the Nations doctors would not be participating in the new Obamacare, and how many patients, many of whom were in his neighborhood had either never had any insurance, or were dropped by their current insurances, or if they had insurance, rates and out of pocket expenditures were increasing dramatically. Physicians that had large practices were dropped by insurance companies due to larger payouts for services, and that a large portion of highly successful Physicians were converting their practices to "concierge" practices wherein a patient paid a yearly fee for all the doctors services in advance. The average annual fee was approximately $1,500.00, an amount very few if any of his neighborhood residents could possibly afford. Instead he sought newly licensed, highly educated physicians who upon interview and submission of written statements seemed more committed to helping those in need than for financial gain. Medicine in the current world was not the most profitable profession. Engineers, electricians, and auto mechanics, often made more money than physicians. Most medical school students had large amounts of money borrowed from student loans which would take years to pay off. Henry told any prospective physician that he would pay off any student loans in addition to a reasonable salary and benefits.

The search for a medical purchasing agent was difficult. Henry needed a well- informed Nurse or Nurse practitioner with at least a Master's degree in marketing to be the person to stock and purchase medications, solutions, laboratory supplies, and all other materials, from bed sheets to microscopes. This person would have responsibility for a team of professionals who would need, demand, and ask politely for materials that would be needed to supply care to patients. He hired a team of head hunters to work with him to interview and review resumes of many people.

Monique Lee Dan an Oriental woman in her late fifties appeared for her interview. She was a graduate of Duke University, attended NY Binghamton University for her nursing degree, and had a Masters in marketing from Harvard. For the past twenty years she had worked as a medical purchasing agent for three major hospitals, and had given five years of her life with a large medical supply corporation. She was divorced and had two married children, both professionals. Born in Beijing China, her parents migrated to the United States in the late 1940's. Her father was a Chinese physician and her mother his assistant. Monique attained United States citizenship in 1970. She graduated both Duke and Binghamton with honors. Her hair was streaked with bands of white intertwined with a disappearing brunette blackness. She wore no facial make-up however, she was strikingly beautiful. Her language was depleted of any accent, and her choice of vocabulary was that of a college professor.

Monique was a thin tall woman who spoke with an air of confidence and presented an extraordinary knowledge of medicine in general, and a thesaurus of medical equipment. Everyone on the interview team was impressed with her forthrightness and commanding ability to present herself as an expert in all that the team was looking for. As she spoke, Henry was pondering if Monique would be his second wife.

Monique working diligently hand in hand with high levels of major medical and drug suppliers had everything installed and supplied in both hospital pharmacies, as well as in the clinics. Henry saw immediately the respect the staff had for her, and his own deep feelings of admiration for her intellect and presence became stronger than he had initially thought.

Monique was not happy with the costs of certain medication supplies that were offered by the American manufacturers. She therefor arranged a trip to go personally to the Beijing House of Medicine, a large supplier of Chinese manufactured drugs. She wished to design a paradigm for the purchase of certain antibiotics, which in her own opinion were being dispensed much more than necessary in the United States. Antibiotic drug resistant diseases were on the upward swing and she felt as did others that the overuses of antibiotics were the cause of these new strains of antibiotic resistant organisms. The Center for Disease Control has already pleaded with United States Doctors to control their use of antibotics to reduce the amount of diseases resistant to them with more arriving yearly. She decided not to spend any more than absolutely necessary for these drug supplies for the pharmacies.

She was also aware that in deference to the Federal Drug Administration's approval of certain derivative compounds that there were additive changes that made these drugs less effective than the original drugs. Generic drugs for antibiotics, eye-drops, steroids, combination drugs, narcotic pain killers and more recently limits to the sleep aid Ambien caused concern in her mind as to judicious purchasing and stocking, as well as complete control of any re-orders when supplies were running low for certain substances.

Monique was met by a Chinese junior administrator for the Beijing House of Medicine who had arranged a tour of their manufacturing plant prior to her meeting with the administrators who would take her orders which were on a massive scale since the pharmacies had not yet opened and their medicine cabinets were empty.

She saw massive production lines in sterile environments. Masked workers were bent over production machinery in which many items such as pills, powders, solutions, capsules, and every from of medical manufacturing imaginable was occurring. Monique was quite impressed. She was not taken into the processing of formulary compounds, or to speak to any of the chemists who were inserting information into the vast display of computers that surrounded a large room. She could observe their work through a large glass window, but had no direct contact with them.

"We mainly produce generic formularies of drugs whose patents have expired," Wang Shu Lee, the company's president of sales told her as they sat opposite each other at a long oak conference table.

"In the American market the health insurance providers demand generic drugs to lower their cost and the cost to the average person. Our generic drugs on the wholesale market are much less costly than any other country in the world." Lee continued.

"Do you not make any original formulations at all?" Monique asked.

"No ma'am we do not. Our labor force payroll is quite low and we do very well financially with the production of only generic drugs. We do however compete with countries like Canada and Israel for the American market, but I tell you, they are far behind us in production."

Monique stood up and walked over to a large cabinet in which she saw capsules and vials of original drugs. "I see you have an exhibit of many popular drugs that have come off patent Mr. Lee. I see;
Azithromycin
Penicillin
Halcion
Ambien

Pred-Forte
Oxycodone
Hydrocodone
Prilosec
Lisinopril
Metropolol
Klonopin
85 mg Aspirin
Motrin, and many ,many others. Are all these off patents?" she asked.
"No," he answered, but we do not offer them for sale, nor do we
manufacture those still on patent.

Mr. Lee opened a large catalogue listing the drugs he offered for
Monique to purchase for the hospital and the clinics. The price for
what she needed was in the millions of dollars.

The crates of medical supplies for the pharmacies were arriving
daily. Bobby Dale, a pharmacist took a vial of Xanax in his hand and
showed Monique a strange list of numbers and characters which were
written in Chinese. Together they looked at other medications which
purchased from a Chinese company offering low prices. They were
drugs not off patent yet they all had the same Chinese lettering.

"We need to have these codes translated for us. Monique called a
Chinese employee into her office who said she spoke fluent
Cantonese and when she looked at the vials, she said that all the
codes were the same; "non-generic, made in Beijing Medicine."
Monique felt that the subsidiary company of the main factory
somehow related to the Beijing Medical Company, however she was
not sure, and the prices for the drugs was very cheap. She passed on
investigating further and continued to unload and supply both the
hospitals and the clinics with the needed medications.

Sitting before Dr. Henry Calico was one of the largest men he had
ever encountered. "May I give you a warm hearted welcome Major
Warren. I am quite familiar with your heroics, and valor both in Iraq,
and Afghanistan. You earned a silver star in each country for your
bravery, and it is good that our country has acknowledged it. I
understand you were a professional football player for a team in the
National Football League, and when the war broke out in Iraq, you left
the team to volunteer for service."

"Yes, sir, that is true, I have had ten deployments. Now I am once
again a civilian looking for a job."

"What type of work have you done prior to this interview?" Henry asked.

"Mostly security work sir, but retired police and firemen are given first crack at these jobs, as well as those who need extra money, and work off shifts. There are many, perhaps hundreds of veterans looking for jobs that do not exist. Many of them still have not received their veteran'0s benefits from the Veteran's Association. One would think that returning veterans would be able to find jobs, even within the government structures but there are none. Faced with similar problems in the post war economy President Franklin D. Roosevelt created the infrastructure jobs that put many veterans back to work. Things like the Tennessee Valley Authority, but today nothing seems to be done. We give billions in foreign aid while many veterans are homeless and starving or suffering from PTSD without care. The VA hospitals do not have available appointments for many months, and I know of at least two vets who took their own lives most likely in complete psychological despair. It is a complete horror sir."

"You seem to be an honest man who has served his country with honor. Let me explain to you what my needs are. I am here in this neighborhood where I grew up and I am completely dismayed and distressed by the conditions that exist. The people do not get medical care, and I am a Neurologist ready to retire. I have made fortunes of money and now I wish to rebuild this neighborhood offering those in need of medical care, rehabilitation, counseling, and whatever else free of charge or at least accepting what can be paid by any insurance or donated. What I fear is the inherent horror of what the neighborhood has become. It is laden with crime, drugs, rape, beatings, and every kind of unlawful activity one could possibly imagine. I need protection for my two new hospitals and the walk in clinics that I am also building. Each facility must be secure and those inside safe. Thus I want to establish a private force of experienced persons, men and women, especially veterans to patrol the neighborhood and be first responders to crime. I understand that very strong arm tactics must be utilized, however, they must be lawful. I sincerely believe that in time the crime can be stamped out. I cannot provide jobs for every resident, but I will be able to supply health, and that is my goal. A healthy body, and a healthy mind will no doubt, I believe improve greatly the quality of life of the residents in this neighborhood. Once the crime is wiped out, I believe retailors will returns thus more jobs will be available. When the criminals are off the streets the community will once again become alive, and this rotting graveyard of depressed humanity will revive itself. Will you help me and create such a force Major?"

"No doubt in my mind sir. I will need to advertise for personnel, do much training, and plan deployments. But, yes, sir, no doubt, I shall be your health warrior."

The men shook hands and Major Warren said he would return within one week with preliminary plans. Henry said his task force would do the advertising for personnel, and let the Major do all the interviewing.

Chapter 12
Transformation

Donald could not stop his legs from moving. Other than the Asperger's diagnosis he had received as a child he acquired "Shaky Leg Syndrome" within the past few years. If he was stressed, and often when he was in a deep sleep, his leg movements did not stop. The movements often wakened him, and others in his office were disturbed by the constant clicking sounds made by his shoes as the sole of his foot tapped rhythmically on the floor. No one would dare address this disturbance to him, but it was often the subject of small gossip. The initial diagnosis was that he was an ADHD child, but his acute vocabulary and ability to express his thoughts coherently changed the Psychiatrists diagnosis. Autism was also considered, but when he was a child it was not a prevalent medical disorder as it had become. Additionally, he was almost too communicative, a direct oppositional manifestation of Autism. Donald was what he was, he understood it, and made the most of his unending bursts of energy.

When he addressed his desire to leave the employ from the Borgosa family, and was given his unconditional release, he needed to re-direct his life. That fact plus Myron's challenge added to his desire to cease the high end criminal defenses, and keep to the law however in a different setting. One evening while sipping some Scotch, he had his television on and he became intrigued with the actress Kathy Bates, playing the role of a store front lawyer, in the series "Harry's Law."

Donald decided to move to New York City, and he bought a condominium on the upper west side, near 57th street and Ninth Avenue. This placed his residence only a few blocks and over the West Side Highway and the Hudson River. The condominium had all the most modern conveniences. There were flat screen televisions in every room, and a spacious den and bedroom. There was an elegant center hallway leading into a large living room space which he had decorated by one of New York's famous interior designers. The second bedroom and second bath were architecturally likened to Roman baths. Each room had complete floor to ceiling windows. Being on next to the top floor of this twenty floor building, on foggy days one could look out the windows and feel they were in the clouds. The building had both an indoor and outdoor pool, a complete health center that manifested the most modern gymnasium. Donald filled the

bar with every type of alcoholic drink any bar in downtown Manhattan might have. His dinner ware, silverware were, table dressings, and accessories were duplicates from his favorite television show, " Downtown Abbey." When the condominium was completely furnished Donald knew it was time for him to search for office space. He did not select the erudite areas of the city and instead he rented a large empty tax payer store, on
First Avenue and 125th street, in the heart of Harlem. It was an abandoned space and needed complete restructuring. However, given his plan, he ordered only the most frugal desks, shelves, and chairs he found in a consignment shop to furnish the office space. On the door, in plain lettering he had the sign painted which indicated only "Don's Law Offices and the hours the office would be open.

He had decided to be an adviser to a group of new attorneys, fresh with their new licenses, and willing to work for the disadvantaged, and not for six figure pay. He desired to change the course of his life and apply his skills to teach new young vivacious dedicated attorney's the law and how to represent those who could not afford to pay the fees of "private attorney's. Donald realized he might get a plethora of unusual cases ranging from domestic abuse, child abandonment, drug dealings, or any type of case that plagued the poor, disadvantaged people who lived in the community.

The next task for him was to hire a secretary and a few attorneys that upon interview with him would impress him.

Donald was sitting behind his desk and Mrs. Bertha Walker was sitting erect in the wooden chair on the other side of Donald's desk. A black woman with silky-smooth hair tied in a knot behind her head. She wore a floral dress with a crocheted collar. Her shoes had the appearance of orthopedic or diabetic special lasts, which she needed apparently to hold her huge sized body erect. Mrs. Walker was a woman in her late fifties, and had served as a secretary in local school for over twenty years. She had no experience in a law office, but her demeanor was calm and her smile was infinitely infectious and warm. She spoke with great clarity and her warmth made Donald feel confident that with little training she would be an excellent choice for his office.

Donald received many resumes from new law graduates and he soon tired from reading them. To break this monotony he decided that in the evening he would visit a night court. He had never in his experiences been in a court with any but the Borgosa clients. This was not to say those persons were the prime clients an expensive attorney would want to represent, especially since Donald mostly knew his clients were guilty, even before he read the charges against them. His job, perhaps his own well- being was at risk with every representation.

The First District Courthouse was an old red brick building on Nassau Street in lower Manhattan. Donald emptied his pockets, took off his shoes and placed his belt on the moving belt as part of the normal security check prior to entering the courtroom. The room was full of people waiting for the judge to enter and proceedings to begin. In the back row were some men and woman who he immediately felt were attorneys looking for cases, for they were the only people in the courtroom that were dressed in other than street clothing, and each clutched a typical briefcase or attaché case in which papers were stored.

The bailiff motioned to the throng of young attorneys indicating that they could approach those seated and ask if any needed the assistance if an attorney. The response of those seated was minimal as these young barristers walked the aisles asking who needed help. They approached who they thought might be able to pay a fee, and only one young man, dressed very conservatively in chino pants, wrinkled and wearing a battered wool sweater seemed willing to represent a couple who had been served with an order to vacate their home. The eviction as the couple briefly explained seemed unlawful to Donald, as the landlord apparently wanted to turn the building in which they had lived for many years into condominiums and needed all occupants to vacate. It seemed the landlord had obtained inspections from the City, and enough faults were found, true or fabricated to give the occupants eviction orders. The elderly couple explained to the young attorney that nothing was found to be at fault in their home and as well in many others. They were in the court to ask the judge for a stay of the eviction and order a reinspection; for everyone felt the initial inspector was paid off by someone in the buildings department of the city.

The claim made by the inspector was that the tenants were conducting actions of a disorderly house. He claimed it was a building in which those persons living were injurious to public health, and safety which constituted a nuisance in the neighborhood. Donald knew the potential ouster was wrongfully taking the property of the tenants by misuse of the law, putting these persons out without consent or compensation in accord with market values of the residences. He was tempted to walk down the aisle and offer his services to the couple, however, he overheard the young attorney state the wrongfulness of the inspector's decree to the city, and Donald was impressed. He was further impressed when the elderly couple stated that they had no funds with which to pay the attorney and the young man waved them off stating clearly and cogently that he would represent them for no fee, in that he was so enraged at the conduct of the inspector and the City of New York's Buildings Department. Donald sat back and spent the evening learning a great deal. When the court was emptied, Donald approached the young man and offered him his office card suggesting that they meet.

At approximately 3:00 P.M. the next day, a young man dressed in a dark blue business suit, shiny loafers, white shirt, and tie, opened the door to Donald O'Leary's office and approached the desk of Mrs. Bertha Walker. He was tall and thin. He had a carriage of self-confidence, and had a slightly unshaven face. His hair was long, over his ears, but brushed into a barber shop façade.

"Hello, how may I help you?" Mrs. Walker asked looking directly into his eyes.

Brad Duncan presented the business card given to him the evening before by Donald at the court. "I'm here to speak to Mr. O'Leary at his request."

"Have a seat young man and I will let Mr. O'Leary know that you are here to see him."

"Thank you," Brad said taking a seat on the wooden bench that was along the wall.

Donald walked out of his office and extended his hand to Brad in a greeting.

"Hey, did you get that eviction order reversed last night?" Donald asked motioning Brad into his office.

"Well, the Judge felt a re-inspection of the building was in order. He said that a variety of old buildings where tenant had pre-World War Two leases and were paying very little in rent in accord with current day fair market values. He felt that perhaps under a new inspection the landlord might be entitled to updating in the monthly rents, but he was not comfortable with a total eviction order. He said some unsavory landlords have done this type of thing in prior cases. Some have won and most lost. Thus his distrust in the original inspection. He also felt that the New York Department of Buildings could be under suspicion in favoring the claims of these landlords, however, he did not extend his comments to the assumption that the inspector had been financially rewarded for filing a report unfavorable to the elderly tenants."

"Good work Brad, sit down and let's talk," Donald said waving to a metal chair in front of his desk.

Brad opened his briefcase and handed Donald a copy of his resume. Without looking at it, Donald placed the papers face down upon his desk.

"I don't need this Brad. I want to know who you are, not where you have been, and I could not be less interested in your college, law school, or your grades, only who you say you are. No one gives a resume to a prospective employer that does not have glowing letters of recommendation or does not have information pertinent to the job that they are seeking. I am looking for two young attorneys who are more interesting than television, who have a commitment to the law, and who are willing to work hard, very hard for cases other attorneys might not even consider. That is why this very austere office is here in this neighborhood. I want to help the attorneys who work from this office to take cases, very difficult one's, ones that require dedication and skill. The people I wish to represent most likely do not have the funds for another attorney, but need great representation."

"But Mr. O'Leary you are an icon in defense law." " Why this?" Brad asked.

"I have all the money I could ever want. After a career defending persons who may in fact not been innocent of the crimes they were charged with I have come to realize that persons who do not have money can be declared guilty because of poor or inadequate representation, and even sent to jail. I may not have that many years left but I want desperately to change my positions. Are you a person who can help me to do that Brad?"

"No doubt Mr. O'Leary, no doubt. I could have sought out an internship or perhaps an associate position in a law firm. I do not want to be some cog in a large wheel of lawyers. I feel I have an independent mind, and being lost in a large firm making faxes, and typing all day is not my interpretation of what I should be doing. I am more than that. I feel deeply inside of me the need to help and your opportunity, if in fact it exists, is what I want to be. I see myself as an attorney, delving into the law, non-specialized, and clearly at this point not very wealthy. I realize I can learn a lot from you, but I do not discount the fact that you might learn from me, I imagine we could easily be in disagreement, and at each other's throats. I see that working here with you will give me the opportunity not to be a clone. I need only enough money to get a place to live, to eat, and to pay for my work expenses. I am a simple man with high ideals, but I do not place myself on a pedestal. You sir have earned the right to be on the pedestal I on the other hand have a lot of land to travel over to hope one day I can get there as well. I do not know if I ever will be a great lawyer, I have no idea if I have the power of mind to be one, but what I do have is the burning desire to try, to try my best, to outshine your own accomplishments in time. That is who I am and I am ready to begin to work right now."

"Let me show you to your desk Brad. Welcome to O'Leary's Law. Your first case file is in the top left hand drawer of your desk. We can talk about it once you are familiar with the details."

Looking at the young woman waiting on the wooden chair in O'Leary's law office, Donald thought "I hope when they bury me they won't be able to close the lid of the coffin because of my erection." The woman looked more like a Hollywood starlet than a young attorney seeking a job. Her hair was a blazing red, turquoise earrings, large hanging from each ear. Her height was about 5'6"and her body completely filled out the anatomical frame. She was wearing a lovely sweet perfume that filled the air of the office with freshness. Her face was well made up with just a slight inkling of freckles underneath. Her cheeks had a slight blush either from makeup or from it being her natural skin tones. In short, she was lovely, but Donald wondered, was she bright and ready to work hard for little monetary return?

"Diane Marley who are you?" Donald asked hoping he would hear words that set him afire.

"Do you want to know who I am as opposed to what I might be able to contribute to your firm?" the young woman responded sitting down placing her papers on Donald's desk

"Both," Donald responded liking her brashness immediately

"What I am is yet for you to find out, What I can do for you is to work hard, make as few errors as possible, win cases, try my best to be friendly and concerned to potential clients, not to pre-judge anyone, and to respect the fact that you have already made up your mind to hire me. The law is not a problem. It is your interpretation of my skill once we begin. I am more than certain that I will not let you down in terms of my effort, win or lose. I give everything my best, and

I know at times that will not be enough. Those are the times I will turn to you for advice. I hope those times are rare."

"Boy, Wow, you are sure confident of everything, aren't you?"

"Yes I am, I do not respect defeat. It comes not circumstantially; it comes from flaws in the work and preparation. I do not make mistakes consciously; they come from unawareness, surprise, and lack of preparation. Only surprise cannot be dealt with in advance, however, surprise can be remedied by more work and planning. That Sir is me. And if you want me, show me where to begin."

Months passed and one evening as Donald, Brad and Diane were going over a file of a potential drug trafficker who had been stopped and searched by the police they were arguing the merits of the case and the potential that the man's civil rights had been abused. The arrest was suspect and the five counts of criminal activity seemed to be an exaggerated response by the Assistant District Attorney. It was three A.M. and all of the team was tired. Five cups of half consumed coffee filled the air with an odor that was familiar but pungent. Brad was sitting on the floor, and Diane had gotten up from her seat to get a glass of water from the cooler. Suddenly, the large front office window crashed and a large black man wearing a hoody and ski mask broke into the office. He raised his gun and without warning shot Donald, the bullet striking Donald in the head killing him instantly. The man ran, as Diane and Brad crawled on the floor to Donald.

"Call 911" Brad shouted trying to cradle Donald's head in his lap. The blood from Donald's fatal wound stained Brad's pants as Brad tried to give Donald CPR. It was to no avail.

"Oh my God what has just happened, Diane cried out. Why? Who would do this? Donald was a Saint in this neighborhood. Look how many people we have helped. Who would do this? It is insane, completely insane.

The para-medics wrapped Donald's body into a body bag. Two men wearing hazmat uniforms inspected the office for clues that both Brad and Diane knew were absent. The men collected pieces of the broken glass, and sprayed the ground outside of the office window and the floor seeking footprints. None were found.

Chapter 13
Guns

Charles Attleboro read the headline on the front page of the Boston Globe his hands shaking, tears welling up in his eyes. "FAMOUS DEFENSE ATTORNEY, DONALD O'LEARY IS KILLED BY UNKNOWN GUNMAN IN HIS OFFICE LAST NIGHT."A secondary story explained that just outside the offices of O'Leary law, the night of the killing, three young teenagers were shot and killed in a drive-by shooting which also killed a man sitting in a car through the driver's window. When the police arrived they concluded that the man in the car was the killer of O'Leary for he was covered with broken glass particles evidently from crashing through the window of the law offices. He had no identity items on his person. The three teens who were killed they concluded were a completely separate incident. Either a neighborhood gang killing or some type of murder involved with drugs. Charles read the article and called Myron, Henry, and Francis. All of them were aware of the horrendous tragedy that had happened to their friend.

"Do any of you have any ideas as to how we could be of assistance in this terrible tragedy?" Charles asked. Henry replied as did the others that they thought they had to let the police do their work, however, Francis suggested that Charles call Donald's office and ask to speak and or meet with the two attorneys that Donald had hired. Charles placed the call and spoke to Mrs. Walker who told him she would pass his request along to Diane and Brad.

Charles was completely upset, enraged, and concerned with all the gunmen entering schools with weapons in the past two years. The horrendous killing in Connecticut, the three college campuses, the movie theater, and multiple other senseless criminal actions brought to his mind that he could attempt to protect all the schools in Boston by paying for the installation of metal detectors in every school. In addition he felt that the parents of every child registering to attend a school in the city should sign an affidavit reveling gun ownership. He knew he might receive resistance from the NRA, but that did not bother him. If a child came from a home in which guns were kept that child would be required to pass through the installed door protection devices, but a metal detector as well, every day. Teachers were alerted to report any type of unusual behaviors of registered children in whose home guns were kept.

Charles thought that every classroom door should have a pull down bullet proof shield that could be activated by the teacher or from the principal's office.

Elementary, Middle, and Colleges should and with his help could have protection by the use of a type of airport security system. This was to be his accomplishment not in lieu of Myron's challenge, but a great deed upon which to spend his money, a charitable accomplishment to protect students. However when his proposal was presented to the greater Boston City Council he was quite surprised at some of the resistance he met. Councilwoman Brenda Fluke presented a case in which she stated that the installation of such devices would infringe upon the civil rights of the students and that she was already in contact with the ACLU in Boston to bring an action against Charles and the Council in Civil Court to prevent the installation of the scanning devices in the schools, and the registration processes.

The American Civil Liberties Union is a group founded in 1920 to protect basic constitutional rights. It provides legal counsel and AMICUS CURIAE,(friend of the court) briefs on important constitutional questions in civil liberties questions cases, such as those involving EQUAL PROTECTION OF LAWS,DUE PROCESS OF LAW, AND THE FIRST AMENDMENT freedoms of speech, press, religion, and assembly.

The Councilwoman thought that the installation of the devices and parent registration was against the constitutional rights of the children, staff, and any visitors in that it involved equal protection under the law. The buildings that were public property, she felt, should be open and available to all with no restrictions although she did understand that past events were horrendous, but preventing persons from access to public places where free speech and freedom of assembly were guaranteed by the First Amendment. Thus she and the attorneys of the ACLU prepared a brief to present to the court establishing their point of view. It contained a summary of the facts, a discussion of the relevant law, and an argument about how the law applies to the facts, as well as the relief sought by each party.

The ACLU position was that the installation and use of "search" devices were an illegal action against the constitutional law of illegal search. Without reasonable cause to expect students, administrators, or teaching staff to be carrying weapons, or having intent to do harm, the devices were not in the public interest. They quoted statistics about the low incidence of crime caused by hidden weapons in schools across the country and felt the "search devices" constituted an invasion of privacy of the school population. They agreed that the few acts that had occurred were egregious to the population of school persons, but considering the many schools both public and private the incidents were small and not significant to place search devices in all schools. They never introduced into the case the 74 school shootings that occurred after the Connecticut massacre.

Charles Attleboro met with Brad and with Diane. Together they discussed the terrible manner and unexpected suddenness of Donald O'Leary's killing. In essence the police had no clue as to who instituted the murder. The dead man found in the car carried no identification, and a facial recognition, fingerprint, and DNA search all proved uneventful and non-productive. The policed concluded that the killer was an illegal and got into the country through criminal passage. They assumed he was a hired killer, but they had no idea who ordered Donald dead, or why. No one would ever know that it was Emanuel Borgosa who feared that Donald had too much information about his Cartel, and might one day under certain circumstances reveal things Emanuel was fearful of anyone knowing.

"I think we have to let the justice system attempt to figure out the perturbing causation of Donald's murder. I wonder if both of you could represent my case against the Boston ACLU?" Charles asked sipping a steaming cup of imported tea.

After explaining his desire to place security screening devices in all Boston schools, Brad asked, "why in the world would the ACLU be against this free protection for so many children? It seems they want to enact constitutionality just to gain some press. I wonder what a poll of parents and school personnel would show in terms of attitude and graciousness for this offer to provide protection to all these schools. Mr. Attelboro, you are not discriminating between public and non-public schools, you are not neighborhood exclusive, you are not suggesting as some now are that specified school personnel be allowed to possess weapons within the school, so again I ask what the hell is up the ACLU's ass."

"Well Brad I am not an attorney, but sometimes those elements in certain groups need to raise a fuss just to keep their own identities alive within the public's view. You can take Mr. Sharpton, Mr. Jackson and other race advocates who will take up basically minor issues that can be readily resolved, and they make large public outcries of racism, often just to keep their public images. My wish to provide protection for children has no negativity as far as I am concerned. But there are those who see security as an infringement on basic civil rights, and for that conceptualization will take a case to a court, waste the time of the court, and argue against the will of the people, at least those persons with whom they have emotionally created a bond without any understanding other than the inflammatory rhetoric blasted over the airways by the lunatic fringe in the organization. We will take this all the way to the Supreme Court of the United States if we have to. Freelance killing, the use of unlicensed and licensed weapons against an unwary public, specifically children is unconscionable and I am determined to do my best to protect the children of my city. Cost is clearly not a factor. " Will both of take the case?"

Brad and Diane sat nervously listening to Wilma Devonshire, the ACLU attorney continue with her presentation before Supreme Court Judge Arlene Walker who sat on the bench of the Massachusetts Supreme State Court.

"...Your honor in May of 2012 Half of Florida's School Districts mislead parents into thinking that providing Social Security numbers was mandatory for students to register in the public school system. We cannot allow districts to give false impressions that Social Security numbers are mandatory for registration. This misrepresentation was ruled illegal by the sitting judge and if in fact it were allowed it would clearly keep school doors closed for immigrant children. Thus once again attempts to keep certain populations of students representing minority groups is thwarted by declaring this practice illegal."

In another case a judge ruled against the plaintiffs in Hillsboro after analyzing data on student achievement and discipline, the ACLU came out strongly against a proposal to place an armed guard in every elementary school. There is little evidence that the presence of school resource officers, armed guards, will take down a potential shooter. The unfortunate truth is that no amount of additional spending can guarantee that shooting incidents will not occur. What if the SRO is not in the area of the school where the shooter is. An increase in police and guards will result in discipline that is more prevalent among minority students. Schools with SRO's have about five times the rate of arrests for disorderly conduct as schools without them. Last year in the killings in Newton Connecticut convinced educators an SRO could not have prevented that horrendous act of an unbalanced mind. Thus your honor we representatives of the Constitution of the United States do firmly believe the placement of SRO officers, security doors and the like do not and will not prevent these types of crimes. What is needed is more education for school personnel, not more arrests of disorderly students, who unfortunately are minority children. Preventing public school children from attending public schools by virtue of a criminal code is not constitutional nor is it an effective means of proper educational philosophy."

"Mr. Duncan are you ready?" the Judge asked.

"Yes your honor, I am ready and I am here to represent my client Mr. Charles Attelboro in this matter.

Brad began. "Students deserve a safe, secure environment to make the most of their learning experiences. In the wake of recent deadly school shootings, as the one in 1999 at Columbine High School in Colorado, Public Schools in the United States have created security measures significantly with devices such as security cameras and electronic identification cards, and SRO's. School's stress better communication between students and school personnel . However, many students, and unfortunately the majority of minority students come to our public and non-public schools without the basic elements of correct behaviors thus leading to disruptions in the classrooms, and a clear and present disrespect for the authority of school personnel. Some psychologists have suggested this lack of respect in the minority communities might be due to the fact that over 73% of the students, especially disruptive students come from these homes wherein no father is present. Bad parenting accounts for a large portion of the problems the school personnel find themselves dealing with.

Some public schools place metal detectors at building entrances to prevent anyone from bringing weapons onto school grounds. To be effective, metal detectors must be monitored at all times by experienced security guards. Hand held metal detectors can be used for random searches for weapons. Surveillance cameras placed around the school grounds, particularly in areas with an increased likelihood of criminal activity, are another common school security method in use. Security measures could become a problem in that they might arouse an atmosphere of fear and repression, however, these factors should be dealt with in terms of education, both to school personnel, students, and parents.

Many schools, however not here in the greater Boston area, have safeguards in place to prevent unwanted visitors from entering the school. At the most basic level visitors who are approved for entry are given badges for identification. Some more progressive schools issue a type of pass that can be scanned against a data base of violent offenders. Often, visitors are placed in a bullet proof glass enclosure while waiting for the scan to be completed.

Electronic locks, both on all school entrances, dormitories, and on classroom doors, are designed to protect students in case of a violent assault on the school. Some schools conduct regular drills simulating armed raids to make certain students and teachers know how to follow proper emergency procedures. Many schools, especially colleges have a warning siren, or cell phone alert to inform the school population of a serious problem.

One non-technical technique is to build strong school communities wherein communication between staff and students is open and comfortable, thus allowing students to be able to alert school personnel about any impending problem. Studies have shown that communication that is honest and without fear of reprisal might be as good as any electronic or SRO protection. School counselors must encourage students to understand the need for security measures, and those measures must be in place while the education process and the extension of communication exchanges take place. It will not happen over- night. It must include all concerned. It is a process that will take time and hopefully create an atmosphere in which violent attacks are less likely to occur. To say that protecting school children from harm is an unconstitutional act, or a racially provoked one is a completely bigoted and narrow-minded viewpoint. Our children are our future and right now they do not score well on international tests of academia. In fact our children scored in 25th place in mathematics, and 28th place in literature. How sad is this your honor? I would hope upon your own review of the facts you will see that Mr. Attelboro is wishing to do the great city of Boston a wonderful service, give its students an amazing gift of education without fear. In order for the United States to remain the greatest nation in the world, we must do a better job of educating our students. It would be a sin to lose the next Einstein, Werner von

Braun, or George Washington, only because a child is afraid to attend school."

Brad sat down and Diane told him he did a remarkable job.

"Mr. Attleboro, Ms. Devonshire I need time to research and review your presentations. I shall have my clerk call you and inform you of when to return to this court for my decision. Thank you."

Chapter 14
Si Hablo Espa~nol

Francis Domingo placed the telephone back onto the glass table on which sat his iced tea, and his current N.Y. Times business section. He read all the N.Y. Stock Exchange reports and knew his fortune was still growing. Tears dripped down his face as Diane Marley told him of the shooting that killed his best friend Donald O'Leary in Donald's office. His home on A1A in West Palm Beach on the Atlantic coast of Florida was a middle sized mansion. With large tall perfectly trimmed hedges alongside the highway to keep the mansion private and protected from the sight of tourist passerby's. The Mansion was set back close to the water raised on strong beams to protect it from the winds and potential hurricanes.

The original mansion was too large and lonely for him. It was spread over 15,000 square feet and decorated in a wide range of styles, from Louis XIV to Swiss Chalet. This was done mostly by his wife, and Francis paid little attention to the design or amenities. His nose was always on the stock market. The house was a morgue to him and he decided to sell it and move to a much smaller home on Biscayne Bay. This home was built around a large open-air central courtyard and was modeled after mansions he had seen in Spain.

The rooms were large but not opulent. He had marble floors throughout the entire house, built some marble columns, and had the ceilings painted in biblical murals.

He sat on the veranda and thought deeply about his dead friend. Francis knew that Donald had made his money defending members of the Borgosa family and when they last spoke, Donald revealed to him that he was going to leave the Borgosa family and begin a free street law firm to represent those in need. He mentioned to Francis that the street law firm was to be his plan in satisfying Myron's challenge, and that Donald pressed Francis to discuss what Francis planned to do.

Francis took a taxi to a club on South Beach.

Since his wife Dorothea had died, Francis was a very lonely man. He enjoyed the Hispanic heritage that was surrounding him in Miami. The Cuban people and the Hispanics that essentially were mainly illegals from either Cuba or other Hispanic countries were an enjoyable source of entertainment for him.

Francis hired a taxi to take him on tour of the Miami Beach area.

The cab driver began to describe the area they were traveling through.

"South Beach, also nicknamed SoBe, is a neighborhood in the city of Miami Beach. It is located due east of Miami city proper between Biscayne Bay and the Atlantic Ocean. It is a retirement community, full of drug dealers, an entertainment center, and a home for the LGBT community. Television shows like the old Jackie Gleason show televised live from here, and today the more current show, Miami Vice is filmed and both brought familiarity and notoriety to the area."

He continued. " It is a major entertainment destination with hundreds of nightclubs, restaurants, boutiques and hotels. I had read in a recent newspaper, a copy of which is in the door for you to read that about 55% of the residents speak Spanish as a first language. About 30% English, Brazilian and Portuguese about I think, and the Brazilians are buying up much property, with cash."

"In about 2009 the ACLU began looking into instances of Miami Beach police targeting gay men for harassment. In order to quell the uprising about to happen, the police chief Noriega hired a lesbian to serve on the Internal Affairs Department. In fact next month will be another Gay Pride Festival which draws tens of thousands of people to this area. We are booming. Gone are the days of Miami Beach being only for the rich and famous, now it is a cacophony of differences. The Fountain-blue Hotel always one of our famous hotels has been completely re-done and addresses tourists as much as any Caribbean Island does."

"Where is your original home sir?" Francis asked.

"I am from Cuba, believe it or not I got into this country about ten years ago on a small boat that was overloaded with too many persons and almost sank. We were escaping the torment and persecution of Castro. Never would I go back."

"You speak English wonderfully," Francis said.

" This was not the case when I arrived, and it is still a major problem, not only here in Miami Beach but all over the country. It is not English that is the prevalent language of natural born Hispanics, from the illegals, the immigrants that migrated, and for most of the older population. Some families prevent their children from speaking

English and insist that they speak only Spanish. I believe this holds many of us back from opportunities in seeking employment."

"But don't the public schools teach English as a second language?" Francis asked picking up the newspaper that was folded in the door pocket.

"The older folks want Spanish to remain the primary language and they look down upon younger persons who speak English," the driver said. He continued, "we need a new policy of immigration in this country, and a demand that the English language be spoken well by all, even as a condition for citizenship."

"How can that be achieved?" Francis inquired, his head spinning with ideas.

We need better education, more education. We have to be able to show that we as a family of Hispanics are American and the beginning way of achieving that is to make Spanish the second language and English the primary language. We are not like the very religious Jews who speak Hebrew. They formulate their own communities and have little to do with the outside world. Hispanics have become almost the largest part of the American population, and as yet we have not assimilated into Americanism as much as we should. This country was discovered by Hispanics, Columbus, Vasco Dagamma, Magellan, and all the other early explorers. Yet, when the colonies were formed most of the persons arriving to begin this country were Europeans, and they made English the language of the country."

"So you believe the lack of speaking English instead of Spanish can hold back achievement for Latinos in this country?"

"No doubt about it Senior. The older patrons of the Hispanic community do not see the need to learn much English, and they speak to their babies in Spanish, as well as rep-remanding some for not speaking Spanish."

Francis sat back in his seat and went into deep thought. He was not surprised at what the driver said, however, he wondered if and how he might help. Then it came to him. He would build a large free Language learning center and advertise it thoroughly through all media. It would be designed with all the latest technology like Rosetta Stone; and employ the most sophisticated language teachers he could find.

"Is there some kind of council that represents the Hispanic population here in Miami Beach?" he asked the driver who was busy giving an oration about the very expensive yachts tied in their slips along the dock.

"Yes," the driver answered. "There is the Miami Beach Council of Hispanic Heritage, and they are associated with the National Council of Hispanics. There is the National Outreach Program for Diversity and the Hispanic Heritage Council, in fact his evening there is an important meeting of the NCLR. You should go, the meeting is about us Latinos uniting against the prospect of cuts to Social Security and Health Programs. Most of our highly elected officials will be in attendance, and you might have the ability to get a sense of the community, and it's needs. This town hall forum will be held in Miami and will bring together Latino seniors and community leaders who are concerned that the U.S. Congress may reduce the modest Social Security, Medicare, and Medicaid benefits that they rely on for most of their income and health care."

Francis was very impressed with his driver's knowledge and he intended to attend the meeting that evening. He still felt that the inherent lack of English language was a main deterrent to the Latinos community being so dependent on entitlement programs for so long.

"Invitamos a damas y caballeros. Estamos aquí para sicuss asuntos de extrema importancia para nuestra comunidad."(Welcome ladies and gentleman. We have serious business to discuss) Francis did not realize that the entire audience and the main speaker would conduct the program in Spanish.

The speaker one, Enrique Gallardo who was the chairman of the NCLR spoke clearly into the microphone. The audience was completely silent and attentive. He spoke;

" The nation now anticipates the recommendations of a congressional super committee charged with negotiating a long-term solution for the federal budget. There is growing concern about the potential effects of cuts made to programs like Social Security, Medicare, and Medicaid that help keep millions of out of poverty.

The speaker noted that older Hispanics are more likely than other seniors to access Medicare with the support of Medicaid, and may experience the worst of the repercussions from proposals to reduce the federal deficit by cutting these programs and Social Security benefits.

The promise of a stable retirement that Social Security offers to millions of Americans and which Is so critical to the Latin community, now and in the future, should never be threatened, especially to reduce the national debt.

In Miami-Dade County Social Security contributes more than $4.1 billion annually to the local Economy by paying benefits to more than 371,000 residents, including 256,000 retirees, 42,925

Disabled workers, and 25,570 children. Social Security serves more than 3.7 million residents
Of Florida and prevents 1,070,000 of them from living in poverty.[2]Continuing, Mr. Gallardo said:
" Latino seniors are most vulnerable to cuts in Social security because these benefits represent all
of their income. Hispanic seniors receive the lowest average benefits due to lower lifetime
earnings. Average yearly benefits for Hispanic seniors are only $12,213 for men and just
$9,536 for women.[3]

Social Security will continue to be needed by future generations of workers. We must take steps
To ensure that these programs are there for our children and grandchildren. Gracias"

Upon the closing of the presentation, the audience rose as one
and applauded and screamed approval, all in Spanish. Not one word
of English was spoken as Francis wandered through the crowd
anxious to be able to speak to Mr. Gallardo. Francis walked towards
him and extended his hand. He chose to speak to Gallardo in Spanish
not being certain the speaker could or would speak in English.
"I am Francis Domingo sir, and I must tell you that although I
completely agree with your presentation, I feel that the preservation of
needs to the Latino community is party their own responsibility. Every
person here in attendance, and everywhere I travel in this community,
I hear only Spanish, no English. It is my belief sir that a large portion
of the Hispanic community would not only have better life time
earnings because of the ability to secure better paying jobs, and not
fall into the complacency of waiting for entitlements fi in fact the
English language were spoken as a primary language. I am not a
racist nor do I wish for Hispanic heritage to dissipate. I think
education and speaking the language of the country will enable youth
to seek higher paying employment. I am aware that we have a Latino
woman sitting on the Supreme Court, we have Hispanic persons in
Congress, and I sir with some others have become billionaires by
getting a good education, by becoming an English speaking
American, and by learning to understand that hard work beats sitting
and waiting for government handouts. Idleness leads to crime and
drugs, and all the negatives built into a society that does not in the
main try with every ounce of strength and intelligence to succeed. I
see young person's sitting around in neighborhoods that in the least

---

[2] NCLR News Release: September 21, 2011

[3] Florida office of Social Security

and with a little bit of concern and effort could be cleaned and renovated. It is my personal opinion as a very successful Latino, a rich banker, in America, that much more effort must be put into converting the primary speakers of Spanish to people who speak fluent English. In order to compete in schools, and in business, speaking English is an essential trait. I want to help. I wish to build and operate completely free of any fee or charges, a large institute for the Development of English Speech in this Latino community. Can you, and the council help me, support me, and give your next presentation in English to demonstrate to your audience that you, a major community leader is going to make the transitional step?"

"Let me get back to you. I wish to speak to other members of the council. I need to think this through with great concern and care."

"May I wish you a good evening and thank you," Francis said shaking Gallardo's hand. But let me add, the Institute will be built regardless of whether I get community support or not. Naturally things will be best with support, but not vital."

Chapter 15
Disaster

Yussaf Yaddalah sat on the floor of the factory smoking an American cigar blowing the ensuing smoke in puffs up into the air. The sound of the 3-D printer was the only sound in the room. The computer operator hunched over the lap top he was working on. The screen displayed a pair of suspenders much like any type one could purchase in a Wal-Mart. The printer was producing the suspenders from the C-4 explosive clay matter. Yussaf needed five pair to be worn by the five men he had selected for the attack on Myron Schwartz's Shalom Village. Once the suspenders were produced the next task was to create the belts, each of a different style and color for the same five men to wear. Finally the shoes were made.

Yussaf had made arrangements for the men to be trained in the skill areas they would need to become part of the work force that Myron's advisers and workman supervisors would soon be hiring. They needed to be trained as carpenters, or electricians, or concrete preparers. Each man was tested to determine which skill would be most appropriate for him to learn and be able to perform without the supervisors or other workman. They needed to learn enough Polish Language to be able to communicate with others working on creating the village. Each man selected was a Jihadist and exceedingly dedicated to the Al-Qaeda cause. They were bright individuals and hard workers. Within the time span available to learn what they needed to know, Yussaf provided transportation for them to arrive at the employment site for skilled craftsmen who were to be selected to work on the project. It was decided that a cell phone trigger for the explosive materials each man wore would not work if in fact they needed to pass through any type of metal detector. Thus the suspenders, the belts and the shoes were coated with a very inflammable chemical that need no more than the light of a cigarette and a cell phone signal to detonate the C-4.

Myron bent over the table on which his crew of engineers had built a model of the project to scale. Johnny Falcone, the chief engineer and supervisor of the project pointed out the features of the miniature village to Myron. Myron was ecstatic. The village materials were being brought to the Auschwitz site by plane, and truck. An airfield had been constructed on the desert floor for the planes to utilize, and new roads were poured to make the desolate area available. Massive amounts of building materials, wood, wiring, steel, concrete, etc., were being delivered to the site twenty four hours each day, seven days per week.

Johnny Falcone sat in his trailer ready to begin hiring workmen. Outside the construction gate, hundreds of workmen stood in long lines waiting for the day to begin, and for assignment to a job site. Abdulah Mustaf, Mohamed Achmed, Benjamin Caleph, Fateh Dehelmud, and Yousef Benjaeed, stood in the line separated by at least ten or twenty men waiting to fill out the employment papers. Each man wore the suspenders, belts and boots made from the C-4 explosive. They were confident they were going to Allah after they completed their terrorist assignments which would come in approximately two months. Each had been assigned a specific area or building in which they would ignite their explosives. The timing had to be exact as they were instructed, and they relished the notion that soon they would be in heaven. Yussaf Yaddalah had promised each man that their families would be well taken care of. As they were standing in the line, soldiers of the Jihad were killing each man's entire family with the belief of Yussaf that if something went wrong and a man was questioned, he might reveal secrets or the names of family members who in turn might be captured, tortured or worse to find out information for the enemy.

Work on the village continued at a fast construction pace. Men worked in three eight hour shifts every day all week, with one shift upon which to eat and rest. By the end of the first month, one church, a post office, and five homes were finished. By the end of the second month five more homes, a synagogue and a meeting hall with classrooms were finished. The plan was to destroy two homes, the post office and the synagogue. At exactly four P.M. on a Sunday early morning, each Jihadist was to go to the selected site and torch the C-4 waiting for the external signal from Yaddalah's cell phone which he would use from an unseen vantage point.

Myron Schwartz came into the construction site riding on a jeep driven by a United States Major from the Department of the Navy, A SEAL. Together they toured the construction site, and Myron was overcome with joy. He was seeing his dream become a reality. Many hundreds of persons had applied for residence in Shalom Village, and their applications were being carefully reviewed by a select committee comprised of men of the clergy, attorneys, social workers and physicians. Every applicant was to be vetted as carefully as if they were running for the Presidency of the United States. Behavioral characteristics, letters of reference from friends, neighbors, family physicians, school personnel and employers were examined with microscopic precision.

Myron stepped out of his tent to smoke a cigarette. He was too stimulated with excitement to sleep. At the same time about one half mile away lying behind a sloping sand dune, Yussaf Yaddalah began to set up his US SOCOM M24, bolt action sniper rifle into its tripod. He knew he was at a safe distance once the explosions occurred, and his jeep, also hidden in thick brush idled silently for his escape. He scanned the area and located Myron smoking in front of his tent. The five Jihadists were in place and at the exact stroke of 2:00 A.M. five thunderous explosions lit the night sky with raging eruptions of flames surging out into the camp. Myron did not scream, his body fell limply to the ground and he never felt the explosive projectile blow his head open splattering his brain matter into the fibrous wall of his tent. Myron fell dead to the ground, never to see fulfilment of his dream.

Yussaf quickly packed up his rifle and sped away from the scene of confusion and the mystification of the event. Men ran with water hoses, and carbon dioxide canisters to quell the intense flames. After finding Myron's body, all wondered if the project would come to a halt fulfilling some prophesy that Auschwitz was never to be a place of peace and life. News reports alluded to the belief that Myron's dream of peace and happiness on these horrid grounds of the past holocaust killings was not to be. Some stories equated the event to American Indian prophesies of the sacredness of their burial grounds.

Chapter 16
Medicine

The Henry Calico Medical Center and Clinics were almost in full operation. Patients were being seen in one of the street walk- in clinics which were staffed by competent Physicians Assistants and nurses. The emergency room of the main hospital was in full operational status. Dr. Bob Waters Chief of Staff sat at his desk concerned about the first statistical analysis of the benefit to risk ratios at the clinics and at the hospital. The risk level was tremendously elevated by the amount of acquired illnesses in patients. There were too many cases of the staph infection Mercer, and other infections. Patients were reported ill or deceased from the use of standard antibiotics which had been used for many years with enormous success. It was known to the medical staff that diseases like Mercer were difficult to cure since the fact of antibiotic resistant microbes like Mercer needed specialized formulations. However, even some children who presented with nothing more than staph infections of their throats or ears were becoming sicker rather than well after the use of some standard antibiotics.

Dr. Waters notified the CDC (Center for Disease Control) and tried to utilize their expertise in attempting to find out what was happening at the Henry Calico institutions. Every patient entering the clinics or the hospital, especially those scheduled for surgery were to be tested for Mercer. The CDC posted notices for Dr. Waters and tried to educate the entering public. The notice indicated that Mercer infection is one the common terms for MRSA (Methicillin- Resistant Staphylococcus Aureus). Initially, Staphylococcal resistance (especially to Penicillin) was unheard of. However bacteria can mutate and develop good resistance against antibacterial medications including Penicillin as well as other antibiotics.

Surprisingly, the causative agent that causes MRSA has natural colonies in the human body. These natural bacterial floras are located mostly inside the nostrils. The skin is also a natural haven for this microbe. They normally stay dormant and do not cause any health problems. When immunity weakens as in HIV/AIDS the microbe becomes pathogenic and very communicable.

Most staph infections are usually treated with Penicillin-class antibiotics, and they are very effective. However with MRSA the antibiotic chosen may be ineffective as the Staph had mutated leading to a very serious illness.

If left untreated or if the causative agent has a strong resistance and virulence, it will cause havoc to other body tissues. Heart valve infection, bone infection, shock syndrome, pneumonia, and most devastating, flesh- destructive complications can occur and lead to death.

The information indicated that MRSA could be community acquired, health care-hospital associated, long term chemotherapy, steroidal therapy or the resultant of an eye "stye" that had become very infected and not treated. Bathroom sanitation was very important as skin contact, poor disinfection, dirty towels, overcrowding, any skin trauma as well as poor personal hygiene and sanitation could all lead to MRSA. The CDC information was targeted to the general public, the clinic and hospital personnel. With early treatment it is curable.

Dr. Water realized that the community the Henry Calico medical facilities were set up to serve were not the communities where good sanitation and prevention from infection were commonplace. Many of the persons living in the area were drug users, alcoholics, and homeless. The conditions of everyday life for many of the people were terribly substandard, however, too many of patients that had been diagnosed early and given Amoxicillin, Azithromycin, Penicillin, and other common antibiotics were not improving and becoming increasingly ill. Dr. Waters feared a pandemic in the community, or at the worst a realization of an epidemic of Staph infections. He needed to consult with Henry Calico.

Henry, Bob Waters, and Dr. Catherine Callen who had come to the hospital from the CDC to help analyze the increasing number of patients that had been treated with early diagnosis of the Staph infection, and had been treated with anti-bacterial medications and who had gotten increasingly ill.

"Dr. Calico did you submit samples of all antibiotics to the FDA for approval?" Dr. Callen asked.

"Why yes we did, in fact the Pharmaceutical company we purchased the medications from is in Beijing China, and they have supplied other hospitals and clinics in the past with no apparent problems."

"Well I do not see any adverse protocols in either patient care, selection of pharmaceuticals, sterilizations, sanitation or any other procedure which would make me suspicious of the spread of the bacteria. I do understand that you service many folks who carry infection however, your staff is quite careful in all respects. It seems that only the Doxacillin, and the Azithromycin are suspect in terms of adequacy of drug verses additives. All drugs contain additives, and some generics pass patent laws by the manufacturer using differing doses of additives which make the particular drug similar to the original but yet different. Other possibilities, and this would be criminal in the least, is that the drug is "watered" down by the addition of non-reactive elements such as sugar or baking soda. If a diabetic for example is given a generic that is laden with sugar it clearly is very dangerous. We need to submit new samples of the two antibiotics to the CDC and the FDA for examination of potency, proper labeling, and additives. Although it could take as long as thirteen years for the FDA to approve a new drug from the laboratory past at least three years of human trials. Doxacillin and Azithromycin had been on the market for human consumption for many years. The Beijing supplier of the antibiotics needed to be contacted and questioned about the purity and efficacy of the two drugs that were purchased from them for the Calico clinics and hospital

Wang Shu Lee answered the call from Dr. Waters while Dr. Callen from the CDC remained quietly on the same line. In addition a conference line had been established with the FDA representative Dr. Phillip Barnes.

"Mr. Lee, we seem to be having an efficacy problem with two antibiotics we purchased from your organization. The Azithromycin and the Doxacillin seem to have less efficacy than the same drugs were are using purchased from an American company. Many patients administered your drugs are not getting the positive effect they should, and in fact some have gotten worse and a few died. We need you to review your manufacturing processes as we on our end have sent recently purchased samples to our FDA for testing if there are any contaminants in these antibiotics. We would appreciate a report of testing that you will do in China of the drugs manufactured by the Beijing laboratories so that we can compare results obtained from our own laboratories."

"Dr. Waters, I can assure you that our drugs are pure and manufactured to the strict guidelines set by your own FDA. The drugs have been on the pharmaceutical market for many years with great success in treating bacterial diseases. I see no reason for us to do any further testing and incur great expense."

"Mr. Lee, this is Dr. Phillip Barnes from the United States FDA speaking. May I inform you sir, that if our testing finds fault with the manufacturing of these drugs, and that changes from our laboratory protocols in your products have caused injury to patients, we shall pursue all international means to close your laboratory, and institute American Federal international laws to hold you and your people responsible under the Freedom of Information Act, and consider a criminal suit to punish those responsible. In fact sir if we find that the drugs were maliciously altered for the desire for profitability at the cost of American lives, we shall consider action against those in fault as a terrorist plot to cause harm to our citizens, thus also to our country. I strongly suggest you get to the bottom of any fault and deal with it promptly. At this time, no American pharmaceutical company, hospital, clinic, or medical provider will purchase any pharmaceuticals from your company. If in fact we find this a purposeful action on the part of your country to cause harm, we shall seek deep and severe sanctions through the United Nations against you. I expect to hear from you within the next ten days."

Wang Shu Lee disconnected the phone call and left to go to the offices of Chi Kahn the Chief Medical director of the Beijing laboratory.

Dr. Barnes explained how the antibiotics were manufactured for commercial use. He said "The procedures in antibiotics manufacturing depend upon whether a product is natural, semi synthetic, or fully synthetic. Natural drugs like the ones in question are made by cultivating microorganisms in controlled conditions and collecting the compounds. The production of antibiotics in all cases requires a sterile environment with constant monitoring to check for signs of contamination that might interfere with the safe production of medications. These drugs were manufactured as a preparation of a culture of organisms, like fungi, that produce antibiotics as a side product. They are grown in large fermentation tanks to keep them reproducing. Everything must be controlled, temperature, humidity, and other conditions. It can take several days to produce an antibiotic broth that needs to be run through filtration systems. So basically antibiotics are produced by a process of fermentation, like good wine, or beer. If any artificial "fillers" are to be added to reduce the efficacy of the antibiotic, they are added after the filtration process prior to the liquid being made into tablets or serum for medical use. Once we re-run the testing we will know if the Chinese manufacturer added fillers to reduce the efficacy of the medications, thereby allowing poorer quality medications to be sold at a much reduced market price. In effect, it is completely unconscionable to think that a manufacturer of life saving drugs would alter them by reducing their efficacy by the addition of fillers."

Dr. Waters ordered no further use of the two suspect antibiotics and within the next month the risk to benefit ratio increased to a much more favorable number. Most patients needing antibiotics were given drugs purchased from manufacturers in the United States. Henry Calico made no objection to the increased costs, and was in a deep depression due to those patients that had died within the treatment protocols of his medical facilities. His initial purpose in establishing these facilities was to help the population of the area and clearly not in any manner to negatively add to the death rate. Adding to his depression was the news of Myron's murder, the destruction of much of Shalom Village and what everyone suspected was a mob killing of Donald O'Leary. He wondered," What is the world coming to when philanthropists who want to do only good are destroyed?" The depth of his depression was elevated when the report from the FDA was placed on his desk and he read, "There is no question that the tested antibiotics were tampered with in production, and because of the addition of filler products, the drugs have little to no efficacy. Thus they could not have destroyed the invasive bacteria, leading to deepening illness or death."

Within Henry's mind came the phrase he swore to upon graduating medical school in the Hippocratic Oath. "Do no harm."

Chapter 17
Safety

Brad, Diane and Charles Attelboro sat nervously in the anti- room of the courthouse after having been notified that the judge had come to a decision and would address the court in a few moments. Wilma Devonshire the ACLU attorney sat in a room next door.

"Everyone is here, please be seated. This case takes on a most serious and debatable issue in our country. It has nothing to do with the second amendment, yes, our populace is given the right to carry weapons. We do not even approach that issue here. I am having the bailiff hand out to each of you a list of school shootings that have taken place in our country since the year 2000. I will say that the earliest record of a school shooting occurred on July 26 1764, in the Pontiacs School Massacre, and school shootings and massacres continue to this very day. To be clear, a school shooting is an occurrence in which gun violence takes place at an educational institution, private or public. A school shooting involves a firearm being discharged at or within a school infrastructure and may refer to incidents of shooting on a school bus or near school property while school is in session. Shootings in the United States have sparked a political debate over whether firearms should be allowed in a school, classroom, corridor, or any other place and if in fact there should be strict gun control. It is debated whether the guns are in the possession of trained staff, a guard hired by the Board of Education, or an administrator, or a teacher. I will address the issue presented in this court after each of you has had the appropriate time to review this list.

A PREPARED LIST OF SCHOOL SHOOTINGS FROM 2000.

Date of incident	Place	Killed	Injured
Feb. 29 2000	Fleet Michigan	1	
May 26 2000	Lake Worth Florida	1	
Aug. 29 2000	Fargo, Mich.	2	
Aug 26 2000	New Orleans		2
March 5 2001	Santa Fe Calif.	2	13
March 7 2001	Williamsport, Pa.		1
March 22 2001	El Cajon, Calif.		5
March 30 2001	Gary, Indiana	1	

Date	Location		
Jan. 15 2002	New York City		2
Oct. 7 2002	Bowie,	2	
Oct. 28 2002	Tucson, Ariz.	4	
April 24 2003	Redding, Penn.	2	
May 9 2003	Cleveland, Ohio	1	2
Sept. 24 2003	Cold Spring Nev.	2	
Feb. 2 2003	Wash. D.C.	1	
May 7 2004	Maryland		4
Oct. 24 2004	Memphis, Tenn.		1
March 25 2005	Red Lake, Minn.	10	7
Sept. 13 2005	Chicago, Ill.		1
Nov. 8 2005	LaJollette, Tex.	1	2
Feb. 23 2006	Rossberg, Oregon		1
March 14 2006	Reno, Nevada		2
Aug. 24 2006	Essex,Vermont	1	
Aug. 30 2006	Hillsboro, No. Carolina		2
Sept 27 2006	Baily, Colorado	2	
Sept 29 2006	Carsen, Wisconsin	1	
Oct.2 2006	Nickel. Penn.	6	3
Jan. 3 2007	Tacoma, Wash	1	
Feb 8 2007	Portland Oregon	1	
April 16 2007	Blocksburgh, Va. (Virginia Tech.)	33	25
Oct. 10 2007	Cleveland, Oh.	1	4
Feb 4 2007	Memphis Tenn.		1
Feb. 5 2008	Baton Rouge, La.	3	
Feb. 12 2008	Calif.	1	
Feb 14 2008	Dekalb, Ind.	6	21
Aug. 14 2008	Federal Way Wash.	1	
Oct. 16 2008	Detroit, Ohio	1	3
Oct 21 2008	Arkansas	2	1
Nov. 13 2008	Ft. Lauderdale, Fla.	1	
Jan. 8 2008	New Castle Rl.		1
Jan. 8 2009	Chicago, Ill.		6
Apr. 6 2009	Hampton, Virg.		3
May 2 2009	Cambdrige Mass.	1	
Jan 16 2009	San Frnacisco,Calif.		3
Sept 3 2009	San Bruno, Callf.		1
Feb. 5 2010	Madison, Ala.	1	
Feb 12 2010	Huntsville, Ala.	3	3
Feb. 23 2010	Littleton, Colo.		2
Sept. 20. 2010	Detroit, Mich.		2
Sept 28 2010	Tex.	1	
Oct. 1 2010	Salinis, Calif.	1	
Nov. 29 2010	Mariette, Wisc.	1	
Dec. 6 2010	Colorado	1	
Jan 8 2011	Omaha, Neb.	2	2
Feb. 12 2011	Placer. Calif.	1	2
March 25 2011	Martinsville, Ind.		1
March 31 2011	Houston, Tx.	1	5
May 23 2011	Pearl City Hawaii		1
Oct. 21 2011	No. Carolina		1
Dec. 9 2011	Tx.		2
Dec.28 2011	Flint Mich.		1
Jan. 10 2011	Houston, Tx.		1
Feb. 27 2011	Wash.		1
Feb. 12 2012	Ohio	3	3

Date	Location		
March 6 2012	Jacksonville Fla.	2	
Apr. 7 2012	Oakland Caif.	7	3
May 26 2012	Chapel hill No. Car.	1	
Aug 16 2012	Memphis, Tenn.		2
Aug. 27 2012	Perryhall, MD.		1
Sept 26 2012	Stillwater, Ok.	1	
Oct 6 2012	Mobile, Ala.	1	
Oct. 16 2012	Fairmont No. Dakota		1
Oct. 21 2012	Los Angeles Calif.		4
Dec. 14 2012	Newton Conn.	28	2
Jan 7 2013	Ft. myers, Fl.	1	
Jan 10 2013	Taft, Calif.		2
Jan 5 2013	St. Louis Miss.		2
Jan. 15 2013	Kentucky	3	
Jan 16 2013	Chicago, Ill.	1	
Jan.12 2013	Houston, Tx.		3
Jan.31 2013	Atlanta, Ga.		2
March 15 2013	Orlando, Fl.	1	
March 21 2013	Southgate, Mich.	1	
April 12 2013	Christiansburgh Va.		2
April 16 2013	Texas	1	
April 16 2013	Grambling Tx.		3
April 8 2013	Cambridge Mass.	2	1
April 9 2013	Cincinnati, Oh.		1
June 17 2013	Santa Monica Calif.	6	4
June 20 2013	West Palm Beach Calif.	2	
Aug. 30 2013	Winston Salem, No. Car.		1
Oct. 4 2013	Pine Hills Fla.		2
Oct. 25 2013	Austin Tx.	1	
Nov 2 2013	Greensboro No. Carol.		1
Nov. 8 2013	Pittsburgh Penn.		3
Nov. 26 2013	Rapid City So. Dakota	1	
Dec. 4 2013	Winter Garden Fla.		1
Dec. 13. 2013	Centennial Col.	2	
Jan 21 2014	West Lafayette Ind.	1	

Judge Arlene Walker sat back in her chair. One hour had passed since she handed out the list of school shootings within the last fourteen years.

"Have you folks read the list?"

"Yes Judge," Brad responded.

"Yes your Honor," Wilma Devonshire responded.

"Good, very good. Now Mr. Duncan after reading this list how does it make you feel?"

"Sick your Honor. I never realized that so many children had been the victims of school shootings. I feel sad, disturbed, and sincerely hope that not only will your Honor rule in favor of my client Mr. Attelboro and his desire to attempt to place a protective shield in our schools, but that you will pronounce that much more should and could be done by others to protect our children."

"Fine."

"And what feelings do you express Ms. Devonshire?"

"Your Honor, I feel the same as Mr. Duncan has expressed, however, I, we, do not think that barriers to our schools should be in place. Nor do we feel that having guns in the school will act as deterrents to these apparently sick minded individuals, be they adults or children. There must be some other way."

"Do you see any commonalities in the list Ms. Devonshire?"

"No, Your Honor. The list is quite diverse. These incidents happen all over our country. Many children have been killed or hurt. I feel the commonality is just that, children are being killed, hurt and victimized by mentally sick individuals."

"The commonality is just that Ms. Devonshire. There is no one particular place, community, rich or poor, many geographical locations. There is no commonality at all except that unprotected children are being killed or hurt in almost every state. There is no pattern to this except that children, teachers, and administrators in most of our schools are open and unprotected targets. The list proves this. I imagine when other countries view our newscasts they can only feel that the United States is a belligerent, hostile and violent nation. Not only have we had our wars fought by adults, we have persons who kill and maim our children. We might be seen as shoddier than those nations we have serious conflict with ideologically. We must protect our children, in any way possible, Thus, I rule in favor of the plaintiff, Mr. Attelboro, and I applaud his desire to make our schools safer. Mr. Attelboro I am proud of you as our city should also be. Thank you."

Chapter 18
Secrecy

Francis Domingo sat in his seat on his private jet squirming and uncomfortable no matter what position he tried to be in. In front of him was a large tumbler of bourbon that he had not touched. No one else was on the plane except for the pilot, co-pilot and Rita the stewardess who had worked for Francis for many years.

"Mr. Domingo is there anything else I can get for you?" she asked seeing that her boss was extremely agitated.

"No thank you Rita, I am just deep in thought. I recently lost two of my best friends, and now as we travel to the Pine Needle golf club in Arizona, I will meet with some others with whom I will have a most serious meeting."

"I am sorry to hear of your loss Mr. Domingo, if there is anything I can do for you please let me know."

The air was smooth and the plane silently glided towards Phoenix and a landing where Francis had a limousine waiting for him to drive to the golf club where he would meet with Charles and Henry. All three friends were emotionally devastated with the deaths of Donald and Myron. Francis' limo pulled up to the drive way of the club. Looking up to the balcony sitting near the rail overlooking the gardens he saw Henry's head, bobbing back and forth as he spoke. Francis imagined that Charles and Henry had arrived before he did and that they were already in thinking modes. Some fundamental suggestions had already been made at the conference call that the three friends had prior to deciding to meet at the club together. Very serious and important decisions needed to be made, and equally severe actions needed to be planned. The deaths of their two friends could not go unanswered. No! He thought, action needed to take place, and he had stopped his initial plans for the English school until the deaths of his friends were avenged.

"Francis should be here soon," Henry said finishing his drink waving to the water for another.

"Yes, I guess any minute, we have some very serious decisions to make Henry," Charles replied.

"We have all the money in the world to acquire anyone, anything in order to avenge them. They were good guys" Charles continued.

"Better than good Henry. How is your hospital project going?"

"We are having some problems with certain antibiotics we purchased from a pharmaceutical company in China. For some unknown reason two of the usual and customary antibiotics used to treat staph infections are not working well. We have the FDA and the CDC investigating the problem now. I hear you were successful in your case against the ACLU in your offering door and window detectors for all the Boston schools. How is that going?" Henry asked.

"We have court permission to begin to install the devices and we are in the process of utilizing some new technology in a variety of test school to determine their effectiveness. I believe that as in some other states, legal action will begin to either arm a certain section of the school administrators, or provide trained security persons to be on campus at all times during school hours. It has worked with reasonable success in some places, and not well in others. The courts will have to ferret out the failures and proceed to a universal plan throughout the country. Devices to prevent outside interference in the safety of children and school personal will be only partially satisfactory. Indeed I truly believe that the installation of these protective devices will reduce any outsider student or adult from acquiring entry into a school, however, there is always the potential danger of an insider creating peril."

"Here comes Francis," Henry said standing and waving hello to his friend.

"Sit down, tell me what you want to drink," Charles said hugging Francis tightly around his body.

"So good to see you guys, even given the horrendous circumstances that bring us together," Francis said as he pulled a chair into place and sat down.

"The events that have occurred as we have discussed on the phone must be attended to," Francis said taking a deep swallow of his beer." To me the killing of Donald and the incident at Auschwitz that killed Myron are unforgiveable, and we need to act."

"Do you have any suggestions," Henry asked.

"Well firstly, I want to take on the case of Donald's murder. I am going to tell both of you information that you never knew. Firstly my real name is not Francis Domingo, it is Francis Correla. My father William Correla, stole passports to come to the United States after being involved in drug smuggling for the Mexican Cartels. I was born in the United States however, my father told me of the Cartels and how they

107

operated. I want to return both to Spain and then to Mexico to become deeply involved with the Cartels. I will begin at the beginning in Barrio Chino in Barcelona, and work my way into the depth of the Cartels, especially attempting to get very close to the head of the Borgosa family in Mexico where Donald had done years of protective business for them. Donald's involvement was to act a defense attorney for them doing his best to represent members who he knew had committed crimes. He was masterful in his trade. For whatever reason, he wanted out of his representation and he told me that the Borgosas gave him a freedom pass. I believe it was a complete farce and that it was they that killed him to protect them in case on some matter or event, Donald would release dangerous information. Death to them is as commonplace as this glass of beer is to me. Within the Cartels there is no honor, only fear, and massive amounts of money.

"I can understand your desire to try to obtain revenge for Donald's killing, however, aren't you placing yourself in a situation of great danger," Henry asked.

"I guess so, but I could never forgive myself for not trying."

"Do you have any connections in Spain?" Charles asked, his brow furrowed into tight wrinkles, his lips pursed into an overbite.

"As a matter of fact I do. There is an old friend, his name is Don Diego, and he has all sorts of connections, especially those in the darkness of the drug trade, and even perhaps in the trade of humans. Spain is only a starting place, I realize that I will most likely end up in Mexico but I need a complete picture. The Borgosa family operates mostly from Mexico, getting product from Spain and Columbia with a very large contingent of persons in the United States. My journey begins at what I believe is the beginning, the heart of the body not the soul."

"Just who is this Don Diego fellow and what are your connections to him?" Henry inquired.

"He is and has been for many years a bartender in a café in the El Raval neighborhood in the district of Ciutat Vella a bar near the port in a very shady part of Barcelona. Francis, when telling me of his father said that was the area in which most of the illegal drugs were loaded on ships, many of which were run by newly arrived Pakistan soldiers. It was where Eduardo, Francis father stole drugs and escaped with his wife ending up in Mexico City eventually working for the Medellin Cartel." "Don Diego is my Godfather, actually great god father and I only met him a few times in my life."

Francis continued. " I think I need to become an insider to finally arrive at my destination of revenge, and that revenge will be to hold a gun in the face of Don Marina Mendes whether I get him in Mexico or Columbia or in the United States. That is my goal. It will give me some peace of mind. I will be finished when I have as well killed Emanuel Borgosa, the current head of the Cartel who is running it like a Mafiosa gang and is so well financed that he lives like a king.

"Holy Shit! Charles said. Are you completely nuts? For God's sake you are going to get yourself killed. I know you and Donald were close, but this, this, is insanity."

"I don't care. I was going to set up a major complex of English speaking schools in the Miami area, and I will do it in time. But this comes first. The English schools are so sorely needed in that community, however, going after that bastard Mendes and getting the world rid of the Borgosa Cartel are projects of most extreme importance. Not only will I eliminate what the FBI has not been able to do, I will get rid of one of the greatest suppliers of illegal drugs to the United States. Thus I hope to protect unknown numbers of kids who might have access to these drugs, as well as the new synthetic cocaine now being sold under false names off the counters of convenience stores throughout the country. I am aware that there might be as many as forty some odd cartels working out of Mexico, and that the border control is offensively horrendous. The cartels have many hundreds or thousands of people working for them. It's an old story, cut off the head of the snake to kill it. More than likely someone else will take over, but I intend to make a dent, a beginning,"

"So what Francis, you get them, what next?" Henry asked. We all know Donald made his fortune working for the Borgosa family, but in recent times he changed. He intimated that he was tired of being a defense attorney for the guilty. After all did he not open the street office with the two new kids, ummm, Brad Duncan and the girl Diane Marley. Before you begin this insane journey at the age of sixty three, I think you should speak to these two youngsters to determine just what Donald's true intentions were. Did he really want out or was this new venture another cover. To me getting out of Borgosa or Mendes control would not be an easy task. There had to be some kind of payoff."

"Maybe you're right Henry, however, I am determined to find the persons or persons who are responsible for Donald's death."

"And what type of protection do you think you will have against getting yourself killed?" Charles asked."

"Simple, my money."

Henry, looking directly at Charles told Francis that they were also going on a journey. They were both going to Poland, to Auschwitz, to try and find out what exactly occurred there, to see if the project could get underway once again, and to hopefully find out who killed Myron.

The three friends raised their glass and toasted their dead friends. Each going into their own golf cart they separated left the club and began their dangerous journeys.

Chapter 19
No Regrets

The trip back to Iran and then to Yemen was long and arduous for Yussaf Yaddalah. Although the trip was carefully planned and help from many al-Qaida cells and sympathizers along his route were generous and helpful, he was spent and his energy level was low. He appreciated the quiet acclaim he received for achieving a goal against the infidel as great as the attack on the Beirut embassy, and the World Trade Tower destruction of 9/11, he knew he could not risk any than his brothers knowing of his achievement. Killing the rich Jew and the symbol of the malevolent village being built by him and his money, were accomplishments never done in prior terrorist attacks. He did not consider himself a terrorist, but a righteous person fulfilling Allah's wishes. He should have been feeling more elated, and he wondered if he was getting ill.

The planning for the event was careful and extensive. Those men chosen to work in the village and wear the explosives were men of God. The C-4 that was produced by the 3-D printer and formed into suspenders, shoes, and belts ignited as planned. The detonation chips within the C4 reacted to his cell phone, and BOOM. His own careful concealment behind the sand dune deep in the underbrush was perfect. The head shot he accomplished in killing the Jew was impeccable. Nothing went wrong, and now he was safe in Yemen. To be assured that he would receive honor for his bold act he had placed a note under the hood of his jeep identifying him as the master of all Jihadists and he was to be honored by all.

He sat on the floor of the cave breathing in the thick fumes of Hashish being emitted from the bongs being used by the members of the council. All bowed their heads in respect for this great man and of his accomplishment. He quietly acknowledged their honor and quietly sat down with new plans for another attack already formulating in his mind.

Fiery pictures of the destruction of parts of Shalom Village were shown on Al-Jazeera, the Arab news network throughout the few days after the attack. Still camera pictures of bloodied bodies, burning buildings, scalded and dead human bodies were strewn over the grounds including a full facial picture of the dead Myron Schwartz. Henry and Charles looked at the scenario holding back the nausea in their throats. Neither man spoke. Henry was reviewing files of mercenaries that had been sent to him from a variety of post war groups in response to the ads he placed in many major newspapers. He asked for experienced men and women of physical strength, full military back-rounds, mission's they had been on and letters of commendation from former employers, or military commanders. The ad gave notice that formal interviews would be held at an office building at JFK airport, and those chosen should be ready to leave the United States within hours of approval to be on the mission. No mention of what the mission was, or how many would be selected was revealed.

Charles had commissioned a private cargo airline to carry to the destination arms, vehicles, RPG's and all sorts of military equipment including miniaturized electronic equipment from tracking devices, listening devices, and the most modern visual transmission equipment available. He had undergone an eye surgery in which an auditory/visual microscopic camera was inserted into the lens capsule of his left eye. With this he could transmit signals to a receiving station. Henry had an advanced pair of Google glasses that could enact anything the most advanced computers might be able to do. They felt they were prepared for their planned mission. The planes landed in Krakow and in the middle of the night, they and their ten well- chosen militant mercenaries began their journey South East approximately 100 miles to the Village site. Charles had contracted with a private drone company to screen the area from the air. Riding in the armored truck behind the steel reinforced and plated range rover were;

Dr. Virgil Sanderson: FBI forensic specialist, specialty, firearms, bomb squad.
Roy Schimmel: Ex Delta Force Sniper.
Edward Hilter: Linguist from Duke University, CIA.
Charles Hemoki: Ex. Astronaut, first to make three month solo journey to Mars orbit.
Gerald Williamson Ex-Navy Seal, ten deployments to Afghanistan.
Ed Gura Ex Navy Seal, Medal of Honor winner.
Dr.Emanuel Martine: Wound specialist.
Wallace Russell: Ex-Navy Seal. Professional photographer.
Arthur Metalonis: Forensic specialist, biochemical materials.
Arika Onkala: Clinical Psychologist, West Point.

The land rover driver was Mohammed Abdullah, an Interpol investigator with thirty years' experience in the trade of secrets, and the driver of the armored truck was Andrea Stutz, an ex-Nazi turned patriot and United States intelligence officer. Stutz served as a double agent and was the oldest member of the team. He had exceptional knowledge of Poland first from his time in the Nazi occupation forces, and then as an SS officer passing secret memos to the Allies for freedom from imprisonment or death.

It was an impressive team of experts all of whom Henry and Charles felt could help them unravel what had occurred at Shalom Village.

The convoy arrived at the outskirts of the deserted village which surrounded the Auschwitz camp 2 which had become a symbol of terror, genocide, and the Holocaust. As each of the experienced professionals stepped out of their vehicles they were overcome with the reality of what had occurred here in earth's hell. They each had studied the history while on the plane, however, being in the actual physical place, made their adrenaline spike.

Dr. Martine spoke to each member of the team as everyone viewed the devastation that had taken place in the village. Although the explosions had taken place weeks before their arrival, the air was stifled with the acrid odor of burning materials and human flesh. Arika Onkala quietly went to each team member reminding them that this place was the hell of World War Two, and once again it was a death camp in modern times. She acknowledged that she had the same overwhelming feelings to the team members, but reminded them all that their mission was to uncover the scheme that caused the destruction and bring those responsible to justice. Roy Schimmel called out, "if I find the mother fuckers who did this, they will all die, not from a quick head shot, but from carefully placed most painful wounds anyone could inflict upon another."

As daylight approached, Dr. Virgil Sanderson split the group into three groups to begin to collect anything that might be classified as forensic evidence. This included, pieces of material, wood, metal, plastic; mud, grass, tree leaves; burnt embers from each of the buildings; any human remains; air samples; fragments of explosives, or any other matter that came into question as possibly being able to give some clue as to what caused the destruction.

"I cannot impress upon each of you that you must not overlook anything. All forensic cases begin at or involve a scene whether it is an extensive area of land as this is or a single item. The collection, identification, recording, and processing of a scene is the most vital aspect of any forensic examination. Since this entire area was quickly evacuated and left unexamined, we are in a fertile domain of evidence. What happened here must be identified, classified, and finalized. That is our first step. So once again, collect and protect every and any item you consider of value. If you have any doubts or questions, please come to me. Each piece of evidentiary material will be sent to the National Crime Laboratory for computer, and algorithm analysis. We shall find out what happened here and who is responsible."

Chapter 20
Spanish Friends and Enemies

Francis Domingo called his wife Marianna and explained to her that he needed to go abroad for his friends Henry and Charles. He said he did not know how long he would be away, but that he would call her periodically. The taxi driver took him to the waterfront and dropped him off at the Costa del Sol bar and grill. He knew he was in the Barrio Chino and that danger lurked everywhere, especially for tourists. The air was filled with the odor of the ocean, salty, full of brine, odors of fish, and rotting metal on the ships that were anchored along the pier. He spotted a large rat walking up a tether rope to the anchor chain of one of the ships. The sky was clear, but in the distance he could see darkening clouds indicating an approaching storm. The dock was busy with workers carrying items off and onto the ships. Most ignored him, however one elderly man approached him, smoking a dank cigar, and said, "I knew your father Eduardo. You are the spitting image of him. He was a good worker, but he got hungry, and could easily have been caught and killed. What brings you home?"

"I have business to attend to. Tell me old man is Don Diego still working in the bar? It is he whom I wish to see?"

"Don Diego only is here some times. Only usually when the market is favorable for commerce, if you know what I mean. He is still the go-between for shipments to Mexico, and the recipient of American dollars. Don Diego has become a very rich man, although his wife Loretta, his fifth wife I admit, is only looking for his money. She is young, beautiful, and very smart. She waits until Don Diego dies. She knows the business very well, and will take it over with the passing of the old man."

"Is Don Diego in the bar now?" Francis asked trying to manage to end the conversation with the elderly man.

"No, however, a shipment comes in tonight from the Arabs, and he will be here to make the transfer. We get the opium form Afghanistan because the American idiots never destroyed the poppy fields. Soon there will be a war between the Arabs, the Columbians, and the Mexicans. Mark my words. The drug kingdom must be ruled by a king, not a bunch of penny pinching men who think they are lords."

"I then shall return this evening to meet my friend Don Diego," Francis said hailing a taxi.

The evening air was wet and chilled as the approaching storm came ashore. Francis walked to the Costa del Sol bar to see Don Diego and to try to gain some type of foothold, some information, some direction as to what his next step should be. He needed to know exactly what was going on, who he must speak to and to let it be known that he was a new trader with unlimited cash to buy merchandise from an approved seller. In order to get inside the trade, he needed to be wanted by the top dealers. To do this he knew he needed to spread money around. He needed information and he felt the best way to get it was to buy it.

Walking into the bar he began to cough and gasp for air. The air was filled with the smoke of marijuana, and it was difficult to see but a few feet in front of him. His body jerked as someone grabbed him tightly around his body and began to kiss him on the neck.

"Pablo told me you were in town and that you would be coming to see me," the raspy voice of an old man spoke loudly into Francis ear.

"Yes it has been a long time you old cockroach," Francis replied spinning out of the grasp of his family friend Don Diego.

"What brings you to this stink hole of a place, my friend?"

"Don Diego, I have a thriving business in the States, buying and selling items that are imported from Mexico, from Colombia. I was taken by the hand of my father to realize the trade was so very profitable. However, I have always dealt as a middle man. I need to get to the top. I have unlimited funds to buy product and only product that is of the highest quality. Our United States markets are being deluged by synthetics made in China, and sold under names that attract kids. The product of the synthetics is legal, and can be purchased over the counter in any store. There is a large undercurrent in the country to legalize more drugs than just marijuana. If this happens, our trade will die out. I need to create a whole new business selling product of only the highest quality and at a very inexpensive price. I know I cannot go directly to the Cartel's, so instead, I came here to attempt to work my way to the top of the trade. Money is the answer, and I think you can get my new business started here in the homeland. Can you tell me who to speak to, and who I can make a connection with?"

Don Diego took a long deep drag on his cigar and turned his head and pointed to a table in a darkened corner of the bar.

"At that table sits Antonio de Torres, and Guarcanagari his aid. Antonio controls the movement of all the product out of Spain and the product is still moved from this port. Things have not changed much since your father's time. Let me introduce you."

Together Francis and Don Diego crossed the crowded floor to the table in the corner.

"Antonio I wish to introduce you to an old family friend. He is actually the grandson of one of our old citizens who no longer dwells here. This is Mr. Francis Domingo. He is a most successful American businessman who is interested in speaking with you about a large expansion of his existing fortune."

Antonio de Torres was seemingly out of place in the old, broken down, decrepit bar. He was extremely well groomed, his chin bore a carefully cut beard, his hair shined in the dark light. Antonio had piercing eyes, a deep blue which betrayed his dark olive skin tones. He wore a suit obviously made of silk, and his nails were perfectly manicured.

Sitting to Antonio's right was a massive bulk of deformed humanity. Guacanagari's hands were knurled with deformities of each finger. His face was covered with some greasy substance with the appearance of suntan solution that had not been rubbed into the skin. His massive body was bent over the table and Francis felt he was observing the Hunchback of Notre Dame. The man was a mixture of human and beast. Francis took a deep breath and sat down at the table with Antonio's approval and invitation.

"What, may I ask brings you back to the roots of your family sir?"

"I am a business man seeking to expand my holdings and Don Diego tells me that you are the person who might set me on the right track."

"And just what track is that Francis? Would you like a drink?" Antonio asked waving for service from one of the beautiful waitresses.

"I am an importer of certain product, and I am running short of supply due to measures exerted by the Government of my country in preventing visiting Mexicans from crossing the borders. Don Diego informs me that you are an exporter, and that we might be useful to one another."

"Yes, Yes, we may be able to do business together Mr. Domingo. If you could, I would like to test a sample of what you consider pure for your needs. Can you bring me one kilo by next week?"

As Francis walked out of the meeting room he approached Don Diego. Took his arm and said, "come with me."

"Come where Diego asked?"

"Just come, now, no questions, we are going to take a small trip."

"A trip to where?" Diego asked.

"We are going to London for some research, now get going."

Together, Francis and Don Diego boarded Francis private jet. He instructed the pilot to head towards Liverpool in the United Kingdom. A young stewardess presented Don Diego with a hot meal and a glass of excellent burgundy.

"Ah, my friend," Diego said letting the back of his lounge chair recline. "You have still not informed me of this sudden journey. Please tell me where we are going and why."

Diego, about a few months ago one of my dearest friends, an attorney, Donald O'Leary was suddenly shot dead in his office. He had recently left the Borgosa family, a cartel in Mexico for whom he was providing very expensive legal services. Donald told me that he had gained release from obligation to the cartel and he was free of having to defend their members, many of whom were United States citizens. He was tired, he was fed up, and he was embarking on a new journey to provide legal assistance to the poor, underprivileged, and needy. I am not certain who killed him however it is my belief that it was someone high up in the order of the illegal drug trade. My mission is to find that person and to revenge Donald's untimely death. I have taken a solemn oath before God to accomplish this mission. Antonio de Torres is my first target, and in getting you out of Spain and away from him and that bar, I have protected you from certain death."

"How do you expect to do this? Antonio is protected not only by the animal Guacanageri, but many men."

"I have a plan which you will soon see. But you my old friend are not to be a part of it. I have purchased a nice home for you in Liverpool where there are many bars, pretty woman, and a nice rest for you for all you have meant to my family. It is time for you live out your life in total and complete comfort."

"You are too kind Francis." Saying this Don Diego fell into a deep slumber and never felt the plane land on the runway of Liverpool John Lennon Airport.

The pilot slowly taxied the plane into the wide open doors of a private hanger and Francis woke Don Diego from his sleep.

"We are here at our destination Don Diego." "Wake up."

Liverpool is a city in the metropolitan borough of Merseyside, England, United Kingdom along the eastern side of the Mersey Estuary. The population is about 500,000. It has always been a major port for trade in the early days from the West Indies, Ireland, and mainland Europe. It was also a link in the Atlantic slave trade. It is an amazing city with infrastructure, culture, museums, music, literature, and tourism. Liverpool was the port of registry for the Titanic a name which was blazoned on the ship's hull. Guinness World Records lists Liverpool as the origin of more hit single music than anywhere else in the world. It gave the world The Beatles, Gerry and the Pacemakers, Echo and many more.

Francis got into a private car with Don Diego and headed towards The Liverpool Knowledge Center. Here was to meet with Dr. Noel Jenkel, a Nobel laureate in chemistry. He had spoken to the doctor prior to landing and explained fully to him what his needs were, and that for the doctor's cooperation, Francis would supply the doctor's laboratory with a gift of $500,000 for research.

The Center was located in a large medieval type castle structure with concrete columns and wide staircases. The massive structure was imposing to say the least, and Don Diego felt a chill run through his body. He wrapped himself tightly in his jacket and followed Francis up the stairs. The large imposing building cast tremulous shadows upon the ground. It was a scene from Frankenstein and Don Diego was fearful he would soon meet the mythical monster.

Francis took the steel knocker in his hand and pounded it against the door. They waited for about a moment, when the large creaky door began to open. Don Diego hid behind Francis fearful of creature would emerge from the door. Much to his surprise, the man answering the knock was dressed in a white laboratory coat. He was short, perhaps some five foot six, and he had illuminating white hair that shone in the moonlit entry as a friendly beacon.

The man wrapped his arms around Francis and the gesture was emphatically and joyfully reciprocated." May I introduce my family friend Don Diego to you Dr. Jenkel?" Warily, Don Diego extended his hand and felt the warmth of the flesh emitting from the outstretched hand of the doctor.

"Come in, come in please gentleman. May I take your coats?"

The three men stood in the middle of a large marble hallway with thick velvet curtains covering all the windows. Above them and extended from a domed ceiling was a crystal chandelier that emitted a constant tinkling of the glass as the chandelier rotated slightly from the drafty hallway. Hallway doors surrounded them, each closed by heavy paneling. The entire center hall looked as if it were secretly kept by ghostly forces.

Dr. Jenkel took Francis by the arm and asked him to "come along." He continued I have what you need in my private laboratory which is set apart from other venues in this place. I do much secret work for the governments of the United Kingdom and the United States. What you ordered and need to continue your quest for revenge as you explained to me is ready for use. However, you will need special protection for yourself, and I have prepared that for you as well. Don Diego must leave us now and he will be taken to his new home.

"Don Diego," Francis said looking his friend squarely in the face. The rest of your life will be completely free of stress and you will have no needs that will not be taken care of. I give these to you. The first is the key to your new home, and the second is a key to a vault in the Royal Bank of England in which you will find money, enough money for your life time. I do not wish you to ever be in need or want of anything. Take the money to a few different banks and deposit it. We shall not meet again. However I presume you will hear of my acts on the news and in the written media. Good luck my friend and God be with you."

Francis hugged his friend and kissed him on the cheek. A servant came in behind them and took Don Diego with him. They walked through hone of the doorways as Francis and Dr. Jenkel walked to the door of an elevator. As the door of the elevator closed behind them Francis felt his adrenaline beginning to rush through his body in anticipation of what he was about to see.

The door to the elevator opened and Francis viewed a large room with about ten persons all in hazmat suits working, bending over tables and microscopes. The room was lit in an eerie light blue incandescent glow from long rows of low hung lamps. One wall above the workers were covered with multiple computer screens flashing and blinking information. The floor seemed to be glassine and shone with a sheen that made walking upon it seem to Francis that it would not hold his body weight and he found himself stepping gingerly as he followed Dr. Jenkel towards another room which was in view through the large paneled glass windows, much the same as in a hospital nursery room through which new parents could see their child. With a key card in his hand, Dr. Jenkel swiped a code box and the door swung silently open. Amazed at what his eyes saw. Francis was in a modern laboratory with what seemed to his uneducated mind, a glimpse of a scene from a science fiction movie. No one spoke, no one turned to see who came into the room. Working people were glued to their tasks. Dr. Jenkel nudged Francis along and they approached a marble topped table on which there were three wrapped boxes. The wrapping was not a normal paper, plastic, or usual merchandise covering. It seemed to be porous and yet solid. The shapes of all three packages were the same and Francis wondered what they were.

"Francis, on this table is your means to complete your journey. Please do not come any closer, unless you don a hazmat suit and mask."

"My Lord, Doctor, what the hell have you created for me?" Francis asked stepping back a few paces from the table.

Francis felt an adrenaline rush and began to breather heavily.

"Francis, are you alright? Your face is flushed and you are sucking in air as if it were going out of style. There is nothing here to hurt you, but surely as I will explain what are in those packages will allow you make the most of opportunity to seek your revenge."

"O.K. Do, what do we have?"

"When you called me Francis you knew my job here in this secret laboratory was one in which I and my fellow workers deal with the world's most deadly bacterium and viruses. It was not a major project for me to create your methodology of ridding the world of some of the most salacious, evil individuals who dwell upon our youth and unfortunate. You are about to do the world a big favor. Ridding the world of evil monsters like Antonio de Torres, Don Marina Mendes, and if at all possible without getting yourself killed, Emanuel Borgosa one would suspect that you should be given a Nobel peace prize. Believe me I fully understand that these missions require the highest level of secrecy. The very fact that you wish to go underground into the narcotic trade den of iniquity astounds me. But I am here to help not to lecture. You have made your choices, in retribution for the death of a dear friend and I support your effort with all my will and energy. Let me introduce you to your weapons of mass destruction."

In each of the packages is one kilo of the purest cocaine ever made. However, they also contain a little kicker, shall we say. Ten thousand to twenty thousand spores of Anthrax are deadly doses whether inhaled or absorbed the skin. A person who is exposed will come down with flu like symptoms and if not treated within twenty four hours respiratory failure will kill the subject. That is why in your country and mine there is always fear of anthrax begin released in large stadiums, i.e. the Super Bowl, the World Series of Baseball or here in Soccer. Distributing the anthrax into the air or even in a ventilating system of a large building would be deadly and devastating. So, what is combined, completely undetected except with certain measuring devices in your package are thirty to forty thousand spores of the anthrax. I imagine when you present your ideal package for trial to Mr. Antonio del Torres, he will open it, taste it, and perhaps with any luck run a line of it to sniff. BOOM! He is dead within twenty four hours, and no one could possible suspect you."

"O.K. Doc, but what if he wants me to try it with him?"

"We have thought of that. Prior to presenting him with the package you will dress into a polypropylene wet suit to protect your body, and you will rub this special invisible glycerin treated cream into any exposed areas of your body, especially your hands, and complete head. This will give you complete protection from exposure. Now you will follow me into my surgical suite where I shall insert a special filter into your nasal cavity to prevent any spores from being inhaled by you. Thus you can freely partake of any testing Antonio wishes you to do. At the same time you should bring a large sum of cash to present to him for him to see you are a serious purchaser of his cocaine."

Chapter 21
Finders Keepers

Dr. Virgil Sanderson wiped the incessant stream of sweat running down his face into his eyes to clear his vision. Both he and Arika Onkala were carefully walking the grounds of the devastated community. They were looking for any evidence of an explosive device, A timer, a trigger mechanism, residue, anything they thought might be of value after testing.

Roy Schimmel positioned himself in the window of the remains of the church to be able to spot any intruders to the scene. He opened his tripod and mounted his sniper rifle with a rotatory mount so as to be able to shoot if necessary in any direction. Gerald Williamson and Ed Gura had the grisly task of examining remains, hands, feet, heads, fingers, and such to gather evidence for DNA analysis. Dr. Emanuel Martine and Arthur Metalonis sought photographic evidence of the massacre and began taking thousands of digital pictures.

The day was hot and humid. Dr. Martine kept announcing to all that they must keep hydrated while searching and seek shade at least for ten minutes for each hour working.

A C-143 cargo plane taxied up to the outside edge of the site and began to unload a portable laboratory, and a trailer in which the team could shower, eat and sleep. Henry and Charles watched as the crew unloaded the temporary accommodations and Henry immediately began to set the laboratory equipment as Charles set up the team's quarters. Each had two assistants, and they worked diligently with increasing fervor, with the incessant burning desire for tho search teams to uncover some evidence upon which they could begin to assign blame for the horrendous act of terror.

Days passed and samples were brought into the laboratory for examination. DNA testing and identification led to many Polish citizens as well as some others from France, England, and Ireland. The Irish were well represented as they felt that their brother Donald O'Leary, although not a part in this project, was in fact a dear friend to the members of the club, and as a whole they considered their efforts to aid in the search for the terrorists was an act of remembrance to Donald.

Arika Onkala was walking slowly looking at the ground when she saw a strange fastener piece on a burnt slab of wood. She bent down, and with her gloved hand she picked it up. At first she could not identify the object, so she walked over to Dr. Sanderson to show it to him.

"If I told you what this is, you would not really pay any attention to it. It is however, the end piece, the fastener to suspenders that some men wear to keep their pants up. It must have belonged to one of the workers here and why don't you bring it to Dr. Calico in the lab for analysis."

"Yeh! Sure," Arika said taking the small object from Dr. Sanderson and began to walk back to the laboratory.

Roy Schimmel's attention was drawn to a dust cloud in the distance. He took out his long range scope and as the vehicle came into range he saw three men dressed in Arabic costumes which he thought strange clothing for Poland. Polish citizens dressed much like persons in the United States. The vehicle stopped on the crest of a ridge and the men conversed intently. Schimmel called for the land rover driver Mohammed Abdullah and for Edward Hilter the linguist to come at once to his post. Looking through the scope Abdullah called out the words he could discern and in Farsi told what he observed to both Schimmel and to Hilter. Hilter began to translate and wrote down on a pad what parts of the conversation Abdullah could distinguish.

"Ah, my brothers....see what our Yussaf ....has achieved....dead many dead...they work.....find nothing...Allah is praised...

Schimmel knew killing the three men would not allow for information to be drawn out of them. He set his rifle for rapid repeated action and three shots rang out, as three men in a jeep feel down. Each had been hit, not fatally, but wounded enough to be recovered and questioned. Schimmel called Gura and Williamson, the ex- Navy seals to go out and retrieve the wounded men.

Henry and Charles heard the shots and each ran out to see what was occurring. On Henry's radio, Schimmel reported the incident and told them that the persons were wounded, and being retrieved. At the same time Arika arrived at the lab questioning the shots still holding the item she found tightly n her hand. Henry had no idea what the item was, but Charles opening his lab coat was wearing suspenders and showed both Henry and Arika that the item she had brought was much the same as his own. The only difference was that the item Arika had brought was somewhat malleable not metallic and this brought questions to Henry's mind.

"Let me have it," Henry said taking the object from Charles and he walked into the lab placing the object on a microscope platform to examine it under high intensity magnification.

"It certainly is made of some strange substance," Henry said as the others watched him bent over his table.

"I want to do an element and mineral scan of this to determine its composition."

Henry placed the object inside the detection device and a printout was produced that indicated, plastic, composition C. plastic binder, solvent of some type, something called (DMDNB), and some odorizer. Henry was puzzled and immediately placed the information on a scanner to send it to the F.B.I. for identification. They all waited impatiently for a reply which took about one half hour. The request was prioritized by Henry and the scan printer started to print. It showed:

The product is an explosive called C-4. It is a common variety of a plastic explosive commonly known as Composition C. It is composed of explosives, plastic binders, plasticizers, and usually a odorizer marker.. The chemical is commonly labeled as DMDNB.C4 is easily manufactured by combining the ingredients with a binder dissolved in a solvent. The solvent is evaporated and the mixture dried and filtered. The final material is an off white solid with a texture similar to modeling clay. It can easily be molded into any shape but needs some type of detonator to set it off. It will not respond to plain heat, or smash. It will respond only to direct intense heat or the combination of heat and a detonator. The detonator can be combined with the composition or C4 can be detonated by remote, like a cell phone.

Henry and Anika as well as Charles were startled by the print out. How in the world could a C4 suspender buckle cause so much damage? It had to be more than a buckle, and clearly more than one person. And who set it off. That question might be answered by the wounded men being brought in by the Seals.

Chapter 22
Beijing

Dr. Catherine Callen of the CDC called Dr. Phillip Barnes at the FDA excited and worried about the findings of baking soda extract as an additive to many of the antibiotic pills that were being used at the Calico hospital and clinics. The additive, an inert substance, did nothing to increase the effective value of the antibiotics, and only allowed for a formulary of deceit. Patients being given the drugs were not getting effective dosages, thus the increasing amount of illnesses and deaths. Dr. Callen called Wang Shu Lee the medical director of the Beijing Pharmaceutical Company from which the pharmaceuticals had been purchased. Years before Henry opened his hospital and clinics, the Chinese pharmacy had sent samples of their products to the FDA for approval of importation. At that time the products received perfect clearance from the FDA. The agency had so many pharmaceuticals upon which they needed to test, it never came about that a re-review of the Chinese products was done for purity of the products and for their efficacy. Thus, the antibiotics were never expunged from purchasing orders. The deletion of the efficacy of the antibiotics was a new phenomenon to the pharmaceutical factories in China who were looking to increase their bottom line without worrying about the consequences to patients.

Wang Shu Lee dismissed Dr. Callen's concerns and suggested that there must have been errors in the testing sequences at the FDA. He suggested that he would personally send a new supply of samples to be tested, and he assured Dr. Callen that the products would be as pure and efficacious as they could possibly be.

Dr. Callen immediately knew Lee would send only the most purified product for testing and she suggested that she and some of her colleagues travel to Beijing instead to tour the facility producing the drugs. There was a long pause on the phone and finally Lee answered that he would be pleased to guide her and her companions on a tour of the facility.

Wang Shu Lee immediately called Dr. Jon Lin and told him to destroy any and all tampered antibiotics as an American team of Doctors were flying to the facility to examine production processing, sterility, and shipping. Dr. Lin gathered all his scientists and called a general meeting of every worker to announce to them that every indication of any baking soda, or materials containing it be destroyed in a large furnace at once. Although the destruction of tampered antibiotics would cost losses of millions of dollars, Wang Shu Lee said that once the intense inspection was over, and the facility cleared of any tampering, other inert substances could be substituted for the baking soda, lower prices, and be able to sell the new product to other hospitals and clinics. He felt that there was an unlimited market for cheap drugs, and that in fact they might investigate how to alter other pharmaceutical products to keep their production costs down and increase the bottom line of profitability. He knew very well of the fallibility and ineffectiveness of the American FDA. Even if a new medication was discovered in an American laboratory it could take years for it to pass all the clinical trials prior to it being distributed for general use. The Americans were much too cautious. In China, money meant everything in the growing economy. He felt China would soon pass the United States as the highest rated economy, and it was being done by deceit of product, not only in the pharmaceutical markets, but in many other areas. The Chinese prided themselves for being able to steal and duplicate American products. This extended into the very secretive manufacturing and design of American weapon systems, space craft, and money laundering. The Chinese government felt quite confident that they were able to steal and build complete replicas of anything, doing it well and very inexpensively in comparison to the prices at origination sources.

Dr. Catherine Callan and Dr. Bob waters from the Calico Center sat quietly as the large new Hainano jetliner, the first non-stop airplane from Boston to Beijing Capital International Airport flew on to China. They might have taken American Airlines, Air France or Air China, however, Henry insisted that they get to Beijing as quickly as possible as his suspicion that Wang Shu Lee would act quickly to cover up any unfavorable methodologies happening at the pharmaceutical plant. Given that the FDA unquestionably said the antibiotics were sub- par in their efficacy, and that baking powder was present in them, Henry was livid to say the least. He would have gone himself had he not been totally involved in Poland with Charles trying to determine what had occurred at Shalom Village and the killing of Myron. However he had full faith in the competence of Drs. Callen and Waters. He also suspected that the Chinese like the Syrians during their chemical weapons inspections would in fact hide or destroy any evidence of tampering. Saddam Hussein had fooled the world by acting quickly to hide his weapons of mass destruction even after chemically killing hundreds of Iraq citizens.

Dr. Walter's and Callen were taken from the airport in a car driven by a Chinese national who did not seem to speak a word of English. Not being certain the driver could understand them, they kept their conversation to mundane issues and they did not mention the reason they had come to Beijing. The car pulled up in front of a large building that looked as if it was designed by Frank Lloyd Wright . It was a twenty floor glass structure with gleaming sunlight shining forming an image of an Egyptian pyramid. As they drove towards the main street known as Xi'anmenst they passed the Beijing Medical College and the Beijing Library. The research pharmaceutical building was South of the Medical building, and the driver pulled into a driveway that curved around through a forest of foliage that was thick and emitting steam that made the driver slow down as the car passed through the fog.

They entered the building and were greeted by a most courteous woman who in fact had their pictures in her hand which she compared to their passport pictures.

"Welcome to the Beijing Collective Pharmacy Doctors. We are happy and hope you had a most pleasant flight. I am to be your guide through our facility and my name is Shue ling. I have instructions to demonstrate to you our complete laboratories, our manufacturing facilities, our shipping department and to answer any questions you may have. We ship pharmaceuticals all over the world and clearly your Dr. Calico had placed an enormous initial order with us and we are most happy to serve him in his endeavors."

They toured the building taking photos on their cell phones, and asked many questions. Nothing seemed odd or out of place. As they approached an elevator, they waked passed a very large steel door on which the international sign for radioactivity was evident.

Dr. Waters asked. "What type of radioactive material do you keep in there? I don't know of any process in the manufacturing of pharmaceuticals that would call for the need for radioactive materials."

"That is our most advanced research facility where we have workers experimenting with radioactive isotopes looking for cures for cancer. It is very dangerous, and Wang Shu Lee would not want either of you to be accidentally exposed to radiation. Thus, it is an area that we cannot visit."

Dr. Callen looked with suspicion and tried to communicate her suspicion to Dr. Waters. However, he was already asking Shue Ling if they could be provided with protective suits as the workers wore, and be able to enter the area.

"Oh no, I cannot do that Dr.," she replied. I am under the most strict orders to keep that area closed to any visitors."

When both Doctor's reached their hotel rooms, each spoke silently with the radio blasting to prevent any hidden microphones installed in their rooms from recording any conversations. Neither thought the radioactive area was truly what the guide described. They decided to take a cab to the American Embassy and have a conversation with the ambassador.

The Embassy of the United States in Beijing is the Administrative office of the United States to China and the seat of China-United States relations. The embassy is in Chaoyang District, Beijing. Since the Embassy is out of the reach of the PRC Government it is restricted territory for any United States intelligence that might be an aspiration of the Chinese. The current U.S. Embassy in Beijing is the second largest US diplomatic mission in the world, after the Embassy of the United States, Baghdad. It is a 5000,000 square foot building, an eight story facility incorporating a full impenetrable glass design on a ten acre lot.

Ambassador Bobby Ling served in the United States Senate for twenty years and was fluent in both Cantonese and Mandarin. The phone rang on his desk and the Marine sentinel told the Ambassador that two American Doctors needed to see him in a matter of extreme importance that was related to illnesses and deaths from imported Chinese medications. A Dr. Catherine Callen was from the CDC and with her were a Dr. Bob Waters from a Boston clinic and hospital being built and run by one Dr. Henry Calico, a millionaire benefactor of a massive medical project for low income and poverty stricken residents of the city.

Ambassador Ling told his security team to show the Doctors into his conference room and that he would be pleased to meet with them.

The Ambassador listened intently to the suspicions of the altered medications and of the increase in illnesses and deaths that occurred in patients prescribed these antibiotics. He picked up his phone and asked his secretary to connect him to the Doctor in Chief of the Federal Drug Administration, Dr. Phillip Barnes whom he asked to check throughout the United States largest medical facilities just who might have purchased these drugs from the Chinese, and if in fact they also saw a pattern of poor recoveries. Given that electronic medical records were being used by all medical facilities throughout the country it took only a few hours for the research to be done.

Dr. Waters and Callen were having some coffee in the cafeteria of the embassy when a guard beckoned them to one again return to the Ambassadors conference room.

"I must tell you that extensive collective proof is on hand all over the country. However, none of the facilities had yet made any connection to altered drugs. The FDA is removing any and all of these drugs purchased from Beijing from usage effective immediately. However our suspicions we need proof. The two of you just finished a tour of the pharmaceutical facility and found nothing errant, correct."

"That is correct Dr. Callen said. However, there was one large area coded for radioactivity that we were not allowed to view. I have no idea what is behind the doors, but I think we need to know, and that we need to know now. If in fact the Chinese are hiding materials that were used to alter the medications within those walls, our proof exists there. We have no doubt the medications were altered, but where. We both think it is in that building, and most likely behind those doors. The Chinese knew we were coming on an inspection tour, and they had time to make the additives disappear."

"I want both of you to return to your hotels and await a call from me. It might not be immediate but I assure you, we will find out what if anything is being hidden or stored behind those doors," the Ambassador said.

The doctors thanked the Ambassador and both felt that he would be able to answer their concerns which now were apparently national concerns.

"How many Chinese operatives do we have working at the Beijing Pharmaceutical factory?" the Ambassador asked Colonel Terrance Johnson, senior officer for covert intelligence operations within the city.

"We have two sir one working as a janitor on the night shift, and one who works as a guard."

Ambassador Ling called Colonel Johnson to his office for a meeting.

"Colonel, we may have a pandemic involving certain medications imported to American hospitals and clinics across the country from the Beijing Pharmaceutical factory. Our people at the FDA have discovered that some antibiotics have an additive of all things baking soda, which is inert but lowers the effective effect of the medication in patients needing them for bacterial diseases. These medications are bought much more cheaply from the Chinese, but are of no value if they are not the prescribed strength. Thus the Chinese are saving production costs and selling below fair market value to increase sales and volume. We know they steal government secrets, plans for weapon systems, and advances in many types of manufacturing prototypes. However, this is abhorrent, selling ineffective medications. It seems that they will not stop at any level if they can gain some type of marketing advantage, but to injure the sick, unheard of, even from them. I mean even during the cold war with the Russians in the sixties, they may have tried to scare us with Cuban missile bases; yet, they under Khrushchev valued life and the living and never used poison gas like the World War One and Two Germans who used mustard gas, and more recently Arshad Baser using Chlorine gas to kill his people. I need positive proof it is the Chinese that are altering these medications, and I want that proof now."

Colonel Johnson asked if he could use the Ambassadors phone. He placed a call and said that he needed three specialists for a covert task that needed to be accomplished within the next twenty four hours.

The plan explained to the three special forces men and which was relayed by wrist phones to Cho Wang Doo, the janitor, and also to Dan Wok, the guard was not complicated. Doo was to approach the main lobby greeting desk attendant and inject him with a powerful anesthetic, Propofol, which would render him unconscious, in seconds, He was to push his body under the desk, and move on. Willie Sam one of the Oriental specialists would be dressed in the guard's uniform and sit behind the greeting desk. Dan Wok would approach the guard in front of the radioactive vault and also inject him with Propofol while he and Luan Chou would take his place. Luan had a Geiger counter under his vest to read radiation levels. He also had a small visual intelligent security device that could be used to gain access to any passwords on vault pass-boxes in seconds. Traditionally passwords are only alphanumeric consisting of letters, numbers, and symbols. Luan's device which read Chinese as well as other languages was a graphical password encoder system designed to implement any password used for security purposes It was a graphical encoder and there was no type of password that it could not decode in seconds. Luan placed the Geiger counter against the door and it did not indicate any level of radiation. As Dan Wok grabbed the fallen guard by his uniform, Luan retrieved the password and began to open the massive vault door. Dan Wok dragged the unconscious guard inside the open vault and closed the door while Luan took pictures of the contents inside the vault.

Within the massive vault were countless rows of shelves each filled with boxes of common named baking soda, and others filled with plastic bags containing many thousands of antibiotic pills as the labels on the boxes indicated. Luan closed the vault door and they placed the unconscious guard on the floor in front of the closed door. They then went down to the front reception desk and retrieved the guard from under the desk and placed him on his chair. The team left quickly, and entered an unmarked car that was running, the driver headed towards the Ambassadors office where they were scheduled to report to Colonel Johnson and the Ambassador.

The pictures were quickly uploaded and sent to the Secretary of Defense and to the FDA, and the Secretary of Homeland Security in Washington.

United States President, Wilma Knoxworthy spoke with deft, hardened tones while addressing Wang Shu Lee.

"Mr. Lee as you can see on your monitor, the United States has incontrovertible evidence that you are selling ineffective medications throughout our country causing harm to persons who are ill, and causing death to some who needed these medications to eliminate certain disease conditions. I need you to understand that no American hospital, clinic, or private practitioner will ever purchase any medical equipment, or pharmaceuticals from China. If in fact we find an influx of these altered medications ever again, we shall destroy the factory. You may take this message to your superiors who I hope will treat you accordingly."

Chapter 23
Information and Travel

A medic was bending down on one knee to dress the leg wound of the last of the three men that Roy Schimmel had shot as they approached the village. Dr. Emanuel Martine was dressing the wounds of the other two men. Edward Hilter, the linguist, began to question the men.

"Why are you men here?"

"Where do you come from?"

"What are your names?"

"Are you from a place other than Poland, your dress would seem to indicate someplace in the Mid-east.?"

"Which of the three of you is in charge?"

"Fuck this Pollyanna shit Hilter, let me at them, I assure you they will begin to talk," Williamson the Navy Seal spoke with mounting anger in his voice.

"You know Williamson, we have found out that torture dies not necessarily bring out the truth. It might bring out what they think we want to hear, but not what the truth is," Hilter replied.

"Bullshit Doc, they will tell me the truth," and saying this Williamson took a propane torch from the top of a table and lit it. He held the blue red flame coming out of the nostril of the torch near one of the intruders crotch, and said, "hey Hilter, tell him if he don't speak now, he will become a eunuch."

"Asshole, put that torch down, these guys won't talk. For Christ's sake many of these nut jobs wrap themselves in explosives and blow themselves up. Frying his balls won't open his mouth, so put the torch down, Hemoki, the ex-astronaut said grabbing the lit torch from Williamson's hands.

The questioning went on throughout the night with no responses from any of the three men. The men in Charles group of mercenaries took turns throughout the night and into the next day with no luck.

"We have to assume they are from one of the mid-east countries, and were here to see if the explosions in the village were successful or if another attack needed to be planned. Who knows, Iran, Palestine, Hamas, Iraq, who knows," Arika said. "We are getting nowhere fast, we need to do something that will loosen their tongues, I have an idea," Virgil Sanderson said. "Give each of them a shovel and lets go outside. I want each of them to dig a hole deep enough for them to stand in with their heads just above ground level. It's an old Indian torture I saw in a movie, or maybe it was an Arab movie, Oh shit, who cares. Let's go. Bury them up to their necks and we disappear. We come back in a few hours to see if their tongues loosen. Sooner or later one of them will crack."

The members of the team went back into the village to resume their search for clues. The finding of the suspender clasp gave them the information that the village was purposefully destroyed, most likely by a band of intruders who were working as skilled craftsmen. "Some type of timing had to be in pace, and they most likely wore C4 on their clothing disguised as elements that were imperious to any search. Then it would seem an outside persons hidden, set off the explosives with a remote device. This was the consensus of the team members. They needed to find the person or persons who had originated the plan. The deaths were numerous, and the property destruction massive.

Gerald Williamson disappeared from the group with whom he was searching for evidence. It was getting dark as the sun was setting. He knew it was going to be only a matter of an hour or so before dark. He was enraged by the three men who were buried neck deep. He had seen too many ugly and outrageous torture and killings of innocent women and children in his deployments to Afghanistan. The terrorists killed at will and doing this they instilled complete terror to the residents of otherwise peaceful villages. He felt deep within himself that the three interlopers were terrorists and that he alone could make them speak. He had no conscious or mindset that might prevent him from acting out as he saw so many of these types kill in rage, laughing as they beheaded innocent people.

Williamson walked into the equipment van and retrieved a large wire cutter. He walked slowly towards the three men and bent down on one knee in front of one of them holding the wire cutter in front of his body in clear view of the buried man. The three men looked at Williamson with fear and apprehension.

"I think it is complete bullshit that none of you understand English. I want you to know that I know who you are. You are ready to die for Allah, but are you ready to endure excruciating pain in his name. To blow yourself up to a quick and painless death as a suicide bomber brings you honor in your sick minds. But I am not going to give you that privilege. One of you is about to suffer a great deal of pain and wish I will kill you, but killing you at least now is not what I have in mind. Please let me demonstrate."

Williamson placed the large wire cutter over the right ear of the man that he was in front of, and without warning, he squeezed suddenly and hard upon the handles of the cutter, lopping off the man's right ear. The man screamed from the fiery searing pain that shot through his face and head. Blood ran profusely from the wound. Williamson took the bloody ear and jammed it into the mouth of the man buried next to the man he wounded. The man spit the bloody ear out and began to vomit profusely. All three men cursed Williamson and he began to laugh hysterically as he approached the second man, cutting off that person's nose. Now all three men were screaming from pain and fear.

"Now you assholes better tell me who is behind this slaughter or I will continue."

The third man who had not yet been assaulted screamed out Yussaf Yaddalah, al-Qaeda group of ISIS. Isis was the new arm of the al-Qaeda militia that was in the process of taking over all of Iraq. They knew that the Americans had mostly left, and that the American president would not bring back armed troops. They had lost over 4,000 soldiers, and American troops had suffered over 100,000 injuries in the long Iraq war. It was time for the ISIS militia to take over the country and become one with Assad of Syria.

"Holy shit, Williamson, what have you done to these men?" Dr. Emanuel Martine asked as he approached the bloodied area.

"I have done what you lily mannered anxious professors have not had the balls to do. I got the name of the person responsible for this mess, and I couldn't care less what happens to these three pieces of trash," Williamson replied standing tall wiping the blood off the cutters against his pants.

"I think that we should call Dr. Calico and Mr. Attelboro and tell them what I found out. I am going to speak to Schimmel, Gura, Russell and Hemoki to see if they would join me in a secret mission if the bosses agree to find this Yussaf Yaddalah guy and bring him in. If we manage to kill him, then all the better. I have to see what the bosses want.

Chapter 24
Sniffer

Francis went back to the bar in the Barrio Chino and told the men that he had purchased it from his friend Don Diego. He told them that he was wealthy and had sent Don Diego to live in a fabulous resort town to live out his days in comfort and pleasure. No one seemed to care. In a first attempt to get closer to the regulars at the bar, Francis told the men that for the next week, all drinks were complimentary, no matter what brands, no matter how much, and no matter to what friends they wished to bring. He knew he needed to prove his wealth, and more importantly he needed a path to Antonio de Torres without any probing or curious questioning from anyone. He let it be known he wanted to see Antonio de Torres in a private meeting.

"I can see that Mr. Torres will meet with you, Poncho Frey said gulping down his drink. I know you have met him before, and he is interested in your business. You will close the bar and meet him at Prento Del Sol where you will be taken into a room for the meeting. You will be searched for guns, and for listening devices. If you have them, you will be shot on the spot. Take a taxi, and be prompt at 8:00 P.M. No phone calls, no visitors to your room, and no conversations on the street."

"I will close and return to my room for a shower and a change of clothing. Tell Mr. Torres that I will bring him a sample of what I seek, and what I seek is to be in quite large quantities for which I will pay with cash."

Francis found that putting on the skin tight polyethylene under suit was difficult. He felt confident that when Torres people patted him down for a weapon they would not feel the suit. To anyone touching him, it would feel like natural skin. He spread the protective gel all over his face, hair, feet, hands, and waited until it dried and became completely invisible. It had no odor and to touch his skin there would be no sensation of a covering. Thus he could easily shake hands with Torres who could not detect anything unusual about the touch of hand to hand.

Francis took the brick of treated cocaine now wrapped in plain paper and hailed a taxi. The ride to Prento Del Sol took about one half hour. Getting out of the taxi he paid the driver and gave him a large tip.

"Senor, this is not a good place to be. It is a center where many bad things happen. Are you sure this is the address you wanted me to take you to?" the driver asked.

"Oh, yes, it is, and thanks you for your concern."

Francis walked down five steps to a brightly painted red door with an ornate knocker attached to it. Looking up he saw some type of camera, most likely he was being viewed by persons inside the building. He tried his best to remain calm, mostly because he did not want to sweat wearing the protective diver suit. The sound of the knocker on the wooden door was loud and reverberated in the hollow of the depressed stairway. The door opened slowly, and Francis saw a giant of a man with an automatic weapon strapped to his back. He clutched the kilo of cocaine tightly in his hand holding it against his side.

"You Mr. Domingo?" the man asked in a raspy voice.

"Yes I am, I have an appointment with Mr. Torres."

"Stand very still and place your package on the floor," the booming voice attached to the giant said.

Suddenly two other men appeared and they ran their hands all over Francis body searching for any weapon or electronic device.

"He is clean," one of the men said to the giant.

"May I pick up my package now? It is a gift for Mr. Torres."

"Go ahead, and follow me."

Together the giant and Francis walked towards an elevator door and the giant pressed the down button. The door opened and they stepped into a large open space that looked like a deserted factory. Across the room sitting behind a large desk was Antonio de Torres. On his lap were two young woman, Francis estimated them at best to be teenagers. They were kissing, and rubbing their hands over de Torres body.

"Enough of that, get out of here, I have some business to attend to," de Torres said to the girls pushing them away from him.

"Ah Mr. Domingo, grandson of Eduardo, son of William and husband of Marianna, Welcome once again. I have traced your career which began with your grandfather, a crook who stole product many years ago. You are a most successful banker, and I have learned you are very wealthy. You see, how much I know."

"I am very impressed Mr. de Torres, very. If you have done a thorough job you know my resources are endless, but I am bored and hungry to earn more, and to be able to provide for a certain population that which they desire. But as I told you, I only deal in product of the highest quality. In fact, here in this paper bag, I have brought you a sample of the quality product I desire. Anything of less quality would not be of value to my clientele. My buyers are all very wealthy and would not expect anything less."

"Well Francis, let us see what you have," de Torres reached out to take the package from Francis. Francis took in a deep breath to try to relax. He smiled and handed the package over to one of de Torres aids who placed it on the desk. With care, de Torres cut the package open and sniffed the white powder deeply. He then took a knife and removed small quantities of the powder and spread it into thin lines on the desk. Let us all enjoy the gift Mr. Domingo has brought to us. Each of the four men bent down holding a straw and inhaled the line of powder closest to him.

"Why don't you join us Mr. Domingo? This is excellent, the best I have ever tried. It will be an accomplishment for my people to duplicate the fine quality of this product."

With great apprehension Francis took a straw and bent down to inhale the tainted cocaine. He had never in any manner used drugs before, and he felt an immediate rush and light headedness. He knew he had to keep control of himself and it was difficult.

"Well Mr. Torres, if you are satisfied, I shall leave you some cash, about $250,000 in American dollars to give you cognizance of my needs and desires for product brought to the United States. There is a timeline. I must receive word that the purified product has arrived in no later than thirty days. Are you able to comply with my wishes?"

"Oh, yes," de Torres replied sneezing as he spoke.

"Then I will leave you in good spirits and return to my home awaiting word from you."

Francis knew he was looking at four men who had less than twenty four hours to live. He departed and took a taxi to the airport to his plane and to give the pilot the information that his next stop would be Columbia. Francis went into his private room and changed his clothing and took a long hot shower. He knew he would have to wait for the nasal cavity implant to be removed, and the fact that it did not cause him any discomfort, he was not concerned about it, and traveling next to Columbia with the two remaining altered packages of cocaine, he hoped he would have the opportunity to use it and the suit once again.

Francis gave the pilot the information to set coordinates for the plane to land at El Dorado Airport in the Columbian city of Bogota, and from there he would travel to Cartagena by car. Even though Bogota was the capital city of Columbia, he had read in his research that most of the illegal drugs passed through the port at Cartagena headed for the United States. Boston, New York, Chicago and especially Miami were the ports of entry for the illegal drugs. From the fields and homes of the Cartels in the mountains, the drugs were carried in many differing ways.

He read that in recent times some phony nuns had cocaine packages inside the habits, school buses loaded with children often were used as drug vehicles, phony copies of major corporation delivery vans like Hess, Exxon, and UPS were duplicated exactly and carried drugs to the waiting ships at the port.

The illegal drug trafficking in Columbia led to the formation of four major Colombian criminal gangs referred to as Cartels. The formation of these large Cartels created a new social class and influenced every aspect of Columbian culture. The Cartels not only fought against the Columbian government but amongst themselves in an effort to increase their own trade and profitability.

It was in the dense jungle laboratories that produced the coca, marijuana and other drugs which were imported in America, Columbia's largest illegal drug market in the world. Given the United States War on Drugs, in the year 2000 Peru passed Columbia as the United States largest provider of coca. In the United States it is estimated that one in six persons had tried Cocaine in their lives. Drug consumption in Columbia and in Europe is less than in the United States. The United States and Columbia signed an extradition treaty wherein any drug dealer caught in Columbia could be extradited to the United State for prosecution, the trade continues to thrive. These facts were imbedded into Francis mind and he needed very much to eliminate the largest Cartel dealer he could to at least make an imprint on his path to the Borgosa family. Columbia was only to be a stop off place for him to once again exert some revenge.

The Medellin and The Cali Cartels were the country's largest and most productive. When he began his journey he had made his target Don Marina Mendes. Mendes had at first been appointed to political office by the liberal leader Luis Carlos Galan, however the prominence of Mendes influence and vast wealth created a major public controversy about his appointment and Mendes was dropped.

He returned to run his vast Cartel continuing to amass fortunes. DEA agents felt that the bosses of the Cali Cartel were vastly wealthier, gentlemen and non-confrontational. The Cali Cartel opened pharmaceutical factories, chemical engineering factories, all as fronts to gain access to the materials they needed to produce the illegal drugs. In effect they were treated in much more subtle and non-confrontational manner than the Medellin Cartel.

In the 1990's the Cartels were somewhat dismembered but men like Mendes survived and continued to pollute Americans. The Medellin Cartel killed thousands of people becoming a ruthless organization that eliminated anyone who attempted to interfere with their business. No objector was safe, no citizen, no politician, and no government official. Francis thought of Greek Mythology, "Cut off the head of the snake to kill it," and the head was Mendes.

As the car rumbled through the rough dirt road which led to the stately home of Mendes, adrenaline was rushing through his body. The situation with de Torres was child's play in comparison to this. Here he was entering into an armed camp of the world's most dangerous criminals, and all he had was cash and anthrax. He wondered how to approach Mendes, and in what manner he could get the maniac to expose himself to the altered drug.

The driver of the car stopped as two heavily armed men stepped out in front of it. Behind them was a massive steel gate which connected to a ten foot high concrete wall covered with flush vines. Francis was once again wearing his undergarment of polypropylene

"You guys need to get out of the car so we can inspect it," one of the men wearing a belt of large caliber bullets around his chest and shoulders.

Francis and the driver got out of the cab and walked to the side of the road. Francis had the paper wrapped package in one hand and his briefcase in the other which was loaded with cash.

The men opened all the doors, looked throughout the car seat and compartments, under the hood, under the car, ad opened the trunk.

"The car is clean, what are you holding in your hands Senor?" he asked Francis.

"What I am holding is strictly for your boss. He is expecting me and he is completely aware of what I bring."

"Give me the package and the briefcase."

Francis handed both to him and watched while he cut into the package with a sharp knife. White powder covered the tip of the knife and the man placed it into his mouth.

"Mm mm! Good stuff, we ain't got nothing like this here senor."

Before the opened the briefcase, Francis asked him to call his boss and get permission to open the case.

"Why are you asking me to do that?" the guerilla said grabbing the case placing it on the hood of the car.

"Because the contents of that case are for your bosses eyes only, and I am certain he will not want you to see the contents of my briefcase. But call him. If you do not and you open the case, I do not want to be responsible for your future," Francis said trying his best to remain calm. It was only money, however, he did not know if the man could be trusted to just grab it and disappear leaving him with no bribe for Mendes.

" Yamana, you watch these two while I go to the phone and make a call to the house," the man with the bullet belt said, waving his arm towards Francis and the driver. He walked up to the gate and picked up the phone. His conversation was not animated as one would see if a person was having an argument, it was placid and calm.

The gate opened slowly and they were waved in. "Do not drive to the main house. You will go to the cottage on the side where the man inside Mr. Silva, Mr. Mendes assistant will meet with you."
The driver did not want to drive any further and he told Francis he would have to walk to the cottage. Before Francis could answer or get into the car, the driver made a rapid U turn and sped away.

"Guess you gotta walk Gringo. Not so far. Walk slowly and breathe deep. The air is hot," Yamana said smiling waving his arm towards the path that led to the cottage.

Francis took the package and his briefcase and began to walk. He wanted to be face to face with Mendes, however, that was not to happen. He needed to convince this intermediate person to allow him to meet with Mendes, so his plan would work with the Anthrax as it did with de Torres and his men. Francis walked slowly sweating profusely with his undergarment clinging to his skin. The invisible cream on his skin created a pooling of sweat as it did not let the extruded moisture from his body to pass through it. Francis began to feel lightheaded and he was still about one hundred yards from the cottage. He blacked out.

Awakening, he saw the blurred image of a man dressed entirely in black sitting on the bed he was laid out on telling him to drink slowly. He took the tip of the cup into his mouth and felt the old water run down his throat. He tried to sit up but his body would not respond.

"Take it easy Mr. Domingo a voice from the black suit said. The heat got to you. Gringos are not used to the heat and humidity of our jungle. I will help you to sit up, take some more water, you are dehydrated."

With the man's help Francis managed to sit up and get his legs over the side of the bed. "Who are you sir, he asked looking around the room for his paper package, and his briefcase. Both were on the floor alongside a wall.

"My name is Alonso Mendoza, and I am Mr. Mendes first deputy. I arrange all appointments for him, I see that he eats well that he has cold baths, and beautiful woman. I am his mind, the caretaker of his body, and his protector. We are aware of your need for exceptional product and also that you met with Mr. Antonio de Torres one day ago in Spain. Unfortunately, that deal will fall through as we have heard that Mr. de Torres has been taken to hospital with a deadly form of Pneumonia and is not expected to live. I also know that you have in your possession most likely in that package a sample of the type of quality product you seek for your very wealthy clientele. With it in your case, which I have not opened would be a down deposit if Mr. Mendes feels he can comply with your needs. Is that all true?"

"Yes it is, unfortunately Mr. de Torres could not meet my qualifiers for the product and it was he who suggested I visit Mr. Mendes. You are correct that the package is a sample, and in that case is a sign of my commitment to acquire product of the quality I seek."

"If you do not mind Mr. Domingo, I will take the package to Mr. Mendes for testing of its quality. I shall return in a few hours. Please make yourself comfortable. With Mr. Mendes approval, I will take your money to him and be able to tell you when and where the product will be shipped."

"Mr. Mendoza, I have travelled a long distance with the hope of meeting with Mr. Mendes myself. Is that not possible?"

"No it is not possible."

"Your man at the gate made a small slit in the package to sample the product. Why don't you do the same. If as I know, you will be rather pleased, So much so that you would want me to present the package and the money to Mr. Mendes myself."

Mendoza took the package off the floor and placed it upon the table. He took a spoon and placed a small amount of the cocaine on it. He then sniffed it deeply.

"My God, this is quite special. I shall bring it to Mr. Mendes at once. Remain here please."

Hours passed and while sipping a cup of iced Vodka, Mendez came back into the room.

"Mr. Mendes accepts your deal and will be able to provide you with as much product soon. We shall take you back to the airport and be in touch with you once you are back in the United States."

"Mr. Mendez, did Mr. Mendes sample the product?" Francis asked.

"I don't know. He took the package into his study and he was there with three other men, one a scientist from the laboratory."

Francis had no way of knowing if in fact Mendes had taken a sample of the altered cocaine himself. If he did, he would be soon dead. Realizing that he was at a dead end, he got into the car which was to take him back to the airport and his plane. At this point he was on his way to Mexico and to Emanuel Borgosa.

Chapter 26
Searching

Yussaf Yaddalah clearly had impressed his elders who elevated him the rank of Captain. His successful destruction of the Shalom Village in Poland was an outstanding achievement. No one had yet heard from the three soldiers who were sent to Poland to review the extent of the damage from the C4 explosives. Realizing that the heat from the cigarette lighters would not be enough to ignite the C4, Yussaf had strung thin nearly invisible detonator wires within the C4 with microchip detonator switches that he could activate from his cell phone which is exactly what he did. He wondered deeply what his next adventure might be. It was time he reasoned to strike the Americans again in their homeland as his people in al-Qaida had done to the World Trade Center buildings on September 11. The Americans were involved with the approaching holocaust in the mid-east with ISIS moving into parts of Iraq, and Putin alongside the edges of the Ukrainian border ready to assault the country and annex more than just the Crimea. The Americans were ready to make a deal with Iran and wondered why the Turks had not yet volunteered any troops. It was a good time to strike in the United States. The people had lost much faith in the voracity of the president and elections were to soon be upon them. The country was clearly divided, and catching them off guard Yussaf reasoned would be easy. But where he wondered, and how? He was presently in the Southern city of Sanaa a stronghold for al-Qaida which unfortunately had been undergoing attacks from the Yemense army and American drones. Some top leaders had been killed in drone attacks, and Yussaf saw an opportunity for him-self to move upward in command. He needed another major attack to gain the influence he needed to be a blessed leader of the cause. It was from the leaders in Sanaa that the famous underwear bomber was trained and the devices made. It was indeed unfortunate Yussaf thought that the man could not carry out his assigned mission.

After much discussion at the site of Shalom village it was decided that three men would go to Yemen and seek out the al-Qaeda terrorist named by one of the captured Arabs, this Yussaf Yaddalah. Dr. Virgil Sanderson, Roy Schimmel, and Gerald Williamson, sat huddled together to keep warm as the Apache helicopter in which they were being transported to Saudi Arabia flew low over the ocean to avoid detection by radar. The three men were to be dropped about ten miles off the coast of Yemen with a raft and they were to paddle their way into the coastline and travel overland to the North-East and enter the city of Sanaa in Yemen. The helicopter hovered over the Archipelago of Socotra and dropped the raft and the three men into the ocean. Socotra is a little known island off the South-west coast of Yemen, isolated from the rest of the world, and it was chosen to be the landing site for the team.

Charles had provided each man with United Nations identifications and international passports. Yemen because of the terrorist activity is basically closed to many tourists, and will not allow anyone with an Israeli passport into the country. Travel to Yemen has been strongly discouraged by the United States due to constant political crisis, threat of terrorist attacks, abductions, tribal violence and general lawlessness. Terrorist groups actively target tourist groups with targeted suicide bombings and armed ambushes occurring yearly.

The raft beached and the men deflated it and buried it deeply into the sand. Each was dressed in moderate western clothing carrying a small pack and a camera. They decided not to take any weapons should they be stopped and searched. The guise was to be three interested scientists from the United Nations seeking interviews to engage in conversations relative to a new plan for peace throughout the country. To do this they needed access, and the passports and papers they carried would they hoped give them such access. They did not fool themselves in the fact that they were stepping into one of the hell holes on earth. But each man was completely consumed with the task of capturing this Yussaf Yaddalah and bringing him back to the destroyed site of Shalom village.

The United States with the assistance of the Yemeni government began massive drone strikes against suspected al-Qaeda terrorists in April 2014 and killed many including some of the leaders of al-Qaeda cells. In one strike as many as 500 men were reported killed. However, a large portion of the Yemeni population is sympathetic or frightened of the al-Qaeda personnel, and information gathering is extremely difficult. Virgil, Schimmel and Williamson after taking the ferry from Socotra to the mainland, Rented a SUV to drive through the mountains to Sana'a the capital of Yemen and potentially the stronghold of the largest cell and fiercest al-Qaeda fighters in the country.

The United States Embassy had re-opened after the attack in 2013, and this was the site that the three commandoes headed for. None of them spoke fluent Arabic, the language of the country, so Williamson suggested they hire a local guide. All three had suspicious feelings about the man, but in effect they had no choice but to use a local to get to their destination. They planned to get rid of him once they entered the main city so that he would not become aware of their final destination.

The route was through the mountains and as they came down a long winding trail ahead of them as a barrier attended by five men with automatic rifles slung on their sides. The driver stopped and opened his window. He spoke to the men and he turned around telling the trio that they needed to present identifications and passports. All three gave the driver the United Nation International passport papers, something which the armed men had never seen before. They ordered everyone out of the vehicle, and forced them to the ground on their knees, hands over their heads.

Gerald Williamson the ex- Navy Seal was closest to one of the men, and in a swift contortion of his body, his arm swung out catching the man behind his knee forcing him to fall to the ground. Within a second, and before any of the other men could respond Williamson had the man's weapon and he opened fire upon the other four killing two and injuring two. Roy Schimmel kicked the first man that Williamson had brought down in his head rendering him unconscious. The driver ran off into the heavily vegetated forest screaming.

"Well we came for action, but I did not think we would come upon it so soon," Sanderson said, gathering up the rifles.

"What the hell do we do with them?" he asked.

"Well we don't need prisoners, and if we leave them they will manage to tell what happened and we will be in a shit of a jam trying get into the city," Sanderson continued.

"No problem," Williamson said as he fired a weapon rapidly killing all the border guards. "No one left to tell the tale, except that is for our driver who we have to find and quiet him. If it gets out that there is a bunch of men seeking some al-Qaeda, then we are going to all die."

Each of the men worked hard dragging the bodies into the forest. They then set out on foot to try to overtake the driver who had run from the scene. After a few hours, they gave up looking and returned to the vehicle to continue into the city on their way to the newly re-opened U.S. Embassy. To himself, Williamson felt in a microscopic way he revenged the Cole which was hit by al-Qaeda while in port. Screw these bastards. All they think of is killing and Americans are their main targets. I would not doubt that they think of ways to get at us every day. Fortunately after 9/11 we have stopped their attacks on us, but we lost people at Benghazi and we have no answers for that. I saw a news release before we left that we got some bastard that we think was involved in the Benghazi attack. I hope they cut his balls off.

The men parked the car one block away from the gate of the U.S. Embassy which was located on Sa'awan Street. Armed guards stood in front of the gate alongside a small hut in which another soldier was speaking on a phone. The three men exited the car and slowly walked towards the gate. When they were within a few feet, both guards shouldered their weapons and asked the men to halt and present identification. Each of the trio produced the United Nations passes and their own passports indicating they were Americans.

"It is essential that we have an opportunity to speak to the Ambassador on urgent business," Dr. Sanderson said pocketing his credentials. The guard inside the hut picked up the phone while looking cautiously at the three men. Then suddenly, a concussive blast occurred and everyone fell to the ground. The car the trio of men had been driving in exploded with a fiery resounding percussion and immense flames. Although they were a block away from the explosion, they could feel the intensity of the fire and their bodies shook from the detonation.

Within moments a group of heavily armed marines came running from within the gated compound with their weapons held in firing positions. They encircled the burning heap of plastic, metal, and rubber, but that is all that remained. Not one person was seen on the street. They scanned the windows of all nearby buildings and found only drawn curtains. The team split into teams of two and began to knock on doors, force doors open, and climb stairs to roof tops, but found nothing.

Dr. Virgil Sanderson waked over to the remains of the car and began to inspect part and particles. Looking underneath the front of the car at the remains of the engine he found detonation portions of a bomb that had been planted under the car. It was his guess that the detonation was set off by a distant detonator igniting the explosive material. He thought that someone knew who they were and just what their mission was. Had they not exited the car when they did. They would all be dead. The gate guard took them into the front hallway of the Embassy and they saw United States Ambassador Wallace Kinsey descending a long spiral stairway, heading towards them.

"Welcome gentlemen and I guess that was some welcome. I am happy no one is hurt. Here in this city we are constantly having suicide bombers, car bombs, and the like." He spoke in a matter of fact manner which disturbed Roy Schimmel.

Each man held out his hand to greet the Ambassador.

"Let us go into my conference room so that you can tell me of your reasons for being here and why, you were targeted for death."

Williamson excused himself asking for the bathroom. Once behind the closed door he placed a coded call to Henry Calico in Poland at the village site. He explained what had occurred and asked how much information they should reveal to the Ambassador who seemed unfazed about their near deaths, and Williamson said that he felt uncomfortable with the man. A long pause and then Henry replied.

"We have no choice but to place trust in the man, after all he was placed in this post by the President, and even though you may have some suspicions about him, realize that he faces terrorist activity all the time. It should not and most likely is not his temperament to get excited or to show emotion. I believe you must tell him all. He might be able to help the three of you, or he may actually try very hard to discourage you. You need to play it out and then speak together as how all of you wish to proceed. I know getting this guy Yussaf is essential to our finding out what happened here at the village, but I would not like any of you to take any very unnecessary risks." The line went dead.

Gerald returned to the conference room to see a soldier talking quietly into the ear of the Ambassador.

"Sit down Major Williamson, your call to Poland is understandable, but I assure you I will do what- ever I can for you once I know your mission. Certainly we here in this building are able to detect any and all messages that enter or leave by virtue of phone, fax, text, etc. We need to have that ability. Like the NSA in the U.S. we monitor all and every type of communication. You were absolutely correct in asking advice from your superior who I understand is a physician whom with a Mr. Charles Attelboro is in Poland at the site of the destroyed village. We know of the incident, and I can assume if I may that your mission here is to attempt to find the perpetrators of that horrendous act. Am I correct in my assumptions?"

Yes," Sanderson replied. "Can you help us?"

"What is your mission? With United Nations credentials, and not just U.S. passports it must something of more than U.S. importance."

Dr. Virgil Sanderson related the entire event to the Ambassador who listened intently to every word.

"Believe me when I tell you that I did not know of your benefactors, your employers were engaging on a project to carry on the work of the village at the Auschwitz grounds. It was my understanding that the fellow one Myron Schwartz, a multi billionaire wanted to create this village of peace to show the world which only God knows is in such horrible shape, that peace can be obtained and people of differing back-rounds, religions, belief systems, can live in harmony. All we have especially here in the mid-east is warring factions, we await Russia to move into the Ukraine, the Chinese and the Japanese are at each other's throats, and it would seem that the United States after its with-drawl from Iraq, and soon to be Afghanistan will have to reassess its own internal feelings about remaining a world power. Iran apparently is going nuclear, and Israel cannot let that happen. I believe your Myron Schwartz was a dreamer, not a realist. However, I give him credit for his efforts."

"Mr. Ambassador, Mr. Schwartz was killed with a snipers bullet into his head. He did not die from the onslaught of the village. Although the village project was clearly targeted by a terrorist group, Mr. Schwartz was singled out for even dreaming that peace could exist. We are here to not only try to reveal which terrorist group blew up the village, but also, and perhaps more importantly to find the killer." Schimmel took in a deep breath after his recitation.

"Mr. Ambassador does the name Yussaf Yaddalah mean anything to you?" Sanderson asked.

"Oh yes, I certainly know of him. We suspect he had much to do with a variety of terrorist actions. We are informed that he has quickly risen to the very top of the ladder in either al-Qaeda or ISIS. The group is here sequestered in Sana'a but we have no information as to where. It could be right here in the city, or in the surrounding mountains. We have not made any direct search for him as that is not our mission, however, I take it that is your mission."

"Yes sir, you are quite correct." Sanderson replied.

"Do you have any suggestions as to how we can either find him or flush him out Mr. Ambassador? Schimmel asked.

" I understand he has great pride in himself, sees himself as a national hero of sorts. I would imagine he goes to public places, not knowing that people like your-selves are in search of him," the Ambassador replied.

"I think you need to split up and go to public places, bars, restaurants, central meeting places, here I have a picture of the man. Study it carefully as he may be in some type of disguise. Many of our men wear thick beards and are hard to distinguish one from the other at a rapid sighting."

"Where to begin is our problem, what specific suggestions can you make sir?"

"Well public places, like perhaps some of our restaurants. He may have a favorite place to be if and when in town. Yes, I think given his bravado he would want to be seen and given praise by the locals. Yes, if each of you go to one of our restaurants, and keep going, he might show up."

"Sir Can you give us some names?"

"Let me think. Many of our restaurants are quite expensive especially the tourist places. I suggest these;

1.Yamal Al-Sham which serves mid-eastern food on Haddah Street where many other restaurants are also located.

2. Al-Shaibani, which also serves mid-eastern food and is opposite the Haddah post office on Haddah Street.

3. Al-Fakher Canteen which serves Yemini food.

Like many places in Yemen especially in Sana'a all these places are under security alert by our state department. Any foreigners visiting these places are at great risk. It does not take much to incite a crowd of men to maim or kill at the slightest provocation."

"Thank you sir," Sanderson said as all three shook the Ambassadors hand and headed out into the street. They could see the rancid smoke still rising from the destroyed car, and a crowd of people stood around it.

"Let's split up and travel to each of these places. If a contact is made, let's say in at least a week, we can contact one another by cell, and arrange a meeting to decide how to handle the abduction," Williamson said.

Sanderson said he would go to Yamal al-Sham; Shimmel was to go to Al-Shaibani; and Williamson said he would go to the Al-Fakeher

Canteen. They shook hands and headed in different directions not knowing what would eventuate.

Chapter 27
Ruins

Henry and Charles sat quietly in the armored vehicle as it traversed the ruins caused by the multiple explosions of the C4. Twenty three workers lost their lives and forty more were injured. Together they managed to bring doctors and medical teams to the site to treat those in need rather than have workers take long journeys. The devastation was horrendous, and each man was in a depression. Both had experienced the ups and downs of business successes and failures however neither had been involved in the mass destruction of property and human lives. Buildings were still smoldering, the air was filled with the acrid odor of soot. The entire work force was in a shut- down mode having been moved by truck to another area some five miles from the village.

Sanderson, Schimmel, and Williamson had been gone for almost one week and neither Charles nor Henry had received any word from them. Both knew these volunteers were in terribly dangerous areas in Yemen and that in effect they were on their own. Neither the United States Department of Defense nor the Department of Homeland Security knew anything of these three men seeking the terrorist that was identified by one of the three men captured and tortured at the village. The name Yussaf Yaddalah was not on any security list, no fly list, nor in any computer file that the U.S. government had. However there was little doubt in Henry or Charles minds that this was the man who was responsible for the terrorist attack upon the village.

As they drove past the destruction each was deep in their own thoughts. Finally Henry spoke.

"Charles, I think we have to begin again. Myron's vision was remarkable in his conceptualization of peace for mankind. If we let this go as a final act of terror, we will not have won, the terrorists will have won, and if they can so easily attack here in Poland on sacred territory, who knows what they are now planning for an attack like 9/11 in the U.S.

Our rebuilding to completing this project will be mud in their faces and prove to them we cannot be defeated. It will give our country the high standing in the world we once had, and it will be an indicator that we are not fearful of the premise that terrorists prey upon, fear itself. It will as President Franklin Roosevelt said after the attack on Pearl

Harbor when he addressed the American people and said" All we have to fear is fear itself." We must not let them take this situation and build upon it. We will rebuild and get the village populated making Myron's vision prevail."

"Henry I agree with you wholeheartedly. We need to think differently. We need to build security, and be certain all our workers are free of any dangerous devices. Just having them pass through security devices as we now know is not enough. We will force them to change completely into work clothing we will provide before they can enter the village to work. We shall build security towers manned by expert marksman. We shall build an invisible electronic fence around the work areas, which will trigger an alarm if anyone breaches the beam. Security is going to be our main thrust.
Let us begin to interview replacement workers, and those who have been injured but ready to return to work will be given first opportunity to do so

The original architectural plans that were presented initially to Myron assured that the tourists visiting the site of the camp would not be interfered with nor altered in any manner. The original train tracks were kept in place, the overhead sign that depicted in German, "work and you shall be free," remained as it was to the millions of unfortunate refugees who enter underneath that sign to meet with death.

To enhance visitation a new tram and moving sidewalk was built to help tourists. More guides were hired to explain the events and horrors of the camp. The housing bungalows were all kept in- tact, thus absolutely nothing in the original camp was changed or disturbed. Shalom village was around the periphery of the camp its nearest site was at least three to five miles from any entity of the original camp.

Soon carpentry saws, hammering, steel clanging, and all types of building clatters were reverberating throughout the village. Four large security towers were under construction manned by ex-military personnel in each corner of the globe. Hundreds of work uniforms, undergarments, and construction tools were brought in inspected and given to workers. All food was inspected and tested for foreign substances. A large medical building was the first to be built by Doctors Henry knew well, with nursing and ancillary staff fully deposed. Although Henry was keenly aware of the problem with the Chinese purchased antibiotics in his clinics and hospitals, he now purchased only from trusted sources. His research with his security people revealed without a doubt the Beijing Pharmacy and others were run and controlled by the Chinese government. That made the Chinese government complicit in the deaths of American sick persons and Henry needed a way to let the Chinese know he knew and would act upon it.

He discussed with Charles how Charles could help him deal with the Chinese when he returned to the U.S., and it was simply to prevent his banks which were now all over the U.S. not to deal with Chinese currency. They intended to speak to Francis as well to do the same in his banks. No transactions with credit cards originating in China, no bonds, no securities, no transactions period. He wanted the Chinese government to hurt, hurt deeply, and he waited for them to come to him with a formal apology made public. Charles thought it a great idea, and texted a message to his board to restrain all monetary transactions with the Chinese Yen at once.

Headlines in newspapers around the U.S., television pundits, and newscasters all carried the story of how the wealthy banker Charles Attelboro, would not allow any of his banks to do any transaction with the Chinese. Charles had released Henry's accusations about the altered medications and spontaneous anti-Chinese groups began demonstrating bringing the attention of congress to the situation. Many in the congress wanted to hurt the declining Russian economy during the Ukraine crisis. These members felt that not trading in the ruble would bring the Russian economy to its knees. It never happened. They also knew they could not stop ISIS economically due to its ever growing wealth, at first stealing some 450 million dollars from a bank. ISIS was well funded by wealthy Arab states especially Libya, and Syria. The finding did not only come from dollars, but also from equipment, weapons and fighters. ISIS was in its way to take over most of Iraq, and the U.S. had no clear plan as how to stop the terrorists or how to prevent a three split of Iraq, or how to stop Syria from providing safe haven for them. Neither Charles nor Henry wanted to get into that mess. They had their work cut out for them and they awaited some call from the three mercenaries as well as from Francis.

As Charles and Henry continued their tour of the wreckage Charles asked Henry what he thought Israel's position was. As far as they knew Myron had consulted with the President of Israel and appeared before the Knesset, Israel's governing body. Some members objected deeply to the making of the death camp an international shrine. They saw the village as something that would bring negative reaction from the haters in the world, something that would re-activate the level of anti-Semitism that always existed.

Others saw it as some type of closure to the memory of the horrors and an enlightened viewpoint of forgiveness keeping in mind that the death camp was just that however, the village would represent a new mind -set that peace could be attained between people of differing cultures and faiths.

Henry thought Myron was a visionary in designing and building the village. The unfortunate explosions they knew were the work of biased hatred for any symbol of less than radical Islam, while none of the ISIS or al-Qaeda personage claimed they had any part of the destruction, it was apparent that they did, and that a leader , this Yussaf Yaddalah was very much a part of the situation. With all their hopes that the three men sent to find him and root him out to bring him to justice, to prove his and his followers hatred was foremost in both Henry's and Charles's minds.

Chapter 27
Long Journey

Francis thought deeply about how to approach the circumstances in Mexico. He wondered if the same ploy representing himself as a wealthy client who wanted to purchase pure cocaine for his wealthy clients, or if this ploy had played itself out. He was on his was to Ciudad Obregon International Airport where the home of Emanuel Borgosa had been built. Borgosa was an extension of the Sinaloa Cartel which was always based in the Northwest of Mexico. It had been founded in the 1970's. It trafficked in illegal narcotics into the United States and Canada. It got South American cocaine, heroin from Asia and produced its own methamphetamine and marijuana. In early 1990 the Sinaloa Cartel filled all voids in trafficking. Until fairly recently it operated with impunity in Mexico as elected officials were bribed, killed or intimidated to leave the Cartel alone.

The Cartel had hundreds of agents in the United States whose job ranged from distribution and organization to production of chemical based drugs like ecstasy to procuring guns from gun shows. These agents were also involved in organized-crime rackets such as money laundering. They had 70 distribution cells spread out over 26 states. Some of the cells were in large cities and some in very small towns.

From mid-2007-2009 an operation by the American government called Xcellerator was put into place to target the Mexican Cartels, especially the Sinaloa which was the largest and most dangerous of all. The program resulted in the arrest of over 750 persons, and seizure of tons of narcotics and $60 million dollars in cash. For a while it severely damaged the Cartel's ability to distribute drugs in the United States and Canada. Emanuel Borgosa initially a small time lieutenant in the Cartel began executing members he considered nonloyal and quickly rose to the top quadrant of the Organization.

Emanuel Borgosa educated at Harvard University in Boston Massachusetts, obtained a Master's degree in Business Administration. He graduated Summa Cum Laud and was considered to be one of the students who would eventually rise to the top of the economic circle in the United States. His first job was as an aid to a U.S. Senator and it was his brilliance that designed a large portion of the Senators campaign during the election cycle. In this position he managed to be known by many top level officials and his sensitivity to people in general led him to an understanding of how much hidden criminality existed within the government.

Emanuel was born in 1964 in the Bronx, N.Y. and his family moved and lived in a four story walk up apartment above a Bodega on Eleventh Ave in Manhattan. The apartment had two small bedrooms, a kitchen, one small half bathroom and no living room. Emanuel's father worked as a laborer and was a skilled carpenter. Emanuel's early child hood was one in which he spent most of his free time after school playing on the streets and he quickly learned about the use of drugs when he was a teenager.

Unlike most Hispanic children he was tall 6'3" and blonde. His skin was a typical brown hazel color and he learned Spanish at the same time as he learned English. In High School he was a typical bully ordering youngsters smaller and not as physically capable as he was to do as he ordered. He did not show much respect for his teachers as he felt that he was smarter than most. Although he was a problem behaviorally, his intellect kept him from being suspended. He felt proud of the fact that his friends, less intellectually talented than he, copied many assignments and test answers from him. This made him a leader, and a person who was respected.

At the age of thirteen he was approached by a man wearing a dark black trench coat, trousers which were not cuffed, and shiny brown pointed toe shoes. He asked Emanuel to walk with him and as they approached a cache in the brick wall of a building the man asked Emanuel in a very low voice if in fact he wanted to earn some money. It was a rainy misty night, and the man had his hat drawn done upon his forehead and the collar of his coat was drawn up his neck making his face difficult to discern.

"What kind of money are you talking about mister?" Emanuel asked.

"I need someone to be a delivery boy in return for twenty dollars for each delivery."

"What do I need to deliver, and where do I deliver it?"

"Look across the street, you see that awning hanging out over the Italian restaurant?"

Emanuel turned his head and saw the restaurant the man was pointing out.

"What do you want me to deliver? A pizza?"

"No, I need this package to be given to man who will come out of the doorway wearing a pair of red sneakers."

Saying this, the man opened his coat and took out from underneath it a square package about the size of T.V. remote. It was wrapped in pain paper, and it had no writing on it.

"What's in the box?" Emanuel asked.

"You don't have to know, just give it to the guy and he will give you some money. I will wait here. Bring the money to me and I will give you twenty dollars."

"No problem," Emanuel said taking the small package and crossed the street.

For the next three years. Emanuel became an experienced delivery boy giving the packages to a vast variety of men, woman, and some older boys. One night, on a full moon, the street was brightly lit. As he crossed the street he drove his finger into the package, and when he withdrew it his finger was covered with a white powder. "Shit," he said to himself, all these years I am carrying drugs to buyers. I need to find out where my distributer gets his to sell, and eliminate him. I won't need a middle man. I need to become the supplier, not the messenger.

At the age of sixteen getting a gun which is what Emanuel wanted seemed to be a difficult thing to obtain. He went to one of his best friends Pablo Estevan who was eighteen and asked him if he knew where he, Emanuel could get a gun.

"What the fuck do you need a gun for?" Pablo asked.

"Because we are going into business."

Emanuel explained what he had been doing for the past few years, and that if he threatened the supplier, he might be able to find out the suppliers source of the packages.

"You are crazy man. You are a little piss pot, Ha , only sixteen and you want to go into the drug business. I tell you that you are nuts."

"Don't screw with me Pablo, can you or can you not get me a gun?"

"Yeh sure, but it will cost."

"How much?"

"About one hundred in cash."

"No problem, when?"

"Tomorrow night, meet me in the school yard at 10:00 P.M."

Emanuel waited with great expectation for Pablo to arrive in the yard. He saw him approaching and his pulse raced and adrenaline poured into his body. Sweat formed on his forehead and dripped into his eyes.

"Hey man, what's up?" Pablo said as he hugged Emanuel round the waist.

"Not much, did you get me what I asked for?"

"Yeh man got it here tucked into my belt in the back of my pants. Nice piece, glock nine millimeter. Full load too."

Pablo reached to his back and pulled a shiny black gun out of his belt and handed it to Emanuel.

Emanuel took the gun into his sweaty hand and turned it around.

"Look man," Emanuel said, how do I shot with it?"

"What? You crazy, you never handled a piece before?"

"No!"

"Alright look, move off the safety, cock it, and boom it works."

"You got the cash amigo?" Pablo asked.

"Yeh! Here it is." Saying this Emanuel took ten ten dollar bills from his pocket and handed them to Pablo.

"What's next amigo?" Pablo asked.

"Tomorrow night I meet my man, you will follow me, and I will get the information that will place us in business."

It was a Tuesday night and Emanuel was to meet his dealer on the corner of Fifty Ninth Street around the corner of Tenth Avenue. The street was lined on both sides with three and four level apartments and was poorly lit. Cars were parked bumper to bumper all along the street. It was 3:30 P.M. and Emanuel waited for the man in the hat. In his front right pocket he felt the hardness of the gun and he kept his hand upon it. A car slowly pulled up double parking alongside a large SUV. The window rolled down and a hand protruded from within the car.

The voice from within the car said," Your receiver is a woman about thirty, red hair, wearing a green shawl around her neck, she is on 11th Avenue waiting for the package."

"Can I ask you a question?" Emanuel said getting very close to the cars window.

"No questions just take the package and be on your way. I will encircle the block until you return with the cash."

"Hey man I have been running for you for three years and I don't even know your name."

"You don't need to know, now get moving."

"Where do you get this stuff from?" Emanuel asked holding his hand firmly on the gun on his pocket.

"Look kid, I said no questions, get going."

"Well to tell you the truth I need to know both your name and more importantly where this stuff comes from," Emanuel said slowly pulling the gun out of his pocket. He placed the gun right into the man's face and once again asked the questions. "Your name and where, or else."

"Fuck off kid, and put that piece back in your pocket."

"Get out of the car, and lay down on the sidewalk on your stomach, now" Emanuel said holding the barrel of the gun even closer to the man's face.

"Out of the car now!"

"Fuck off kid, and get moving."

Emanuel released the safety, cocked the barrel and shot into the man's thigh. The man screamed and bent over clutching his leg. You little prick, why did you do that?"

"If you don't get out and tell me what I want to know, you're a dead man, now get moving."

Laying on the sidewalk, the man looked at Emanuel and screamed out a litany of curses.

"For the last time, your name and where you get this stuff from."

"My name is Danny and the shop is on Delancy Street, lower East side, a shoe store, ask for Ronaldo.

Neither Emanuel nor Danny realized that the bullet had hit and severed the Femoral Artery in the man's leg. The blood was spurting out of the wound and neither knew Danny would bleed out in a matter of minutes. Together they got into the bleeding man's car and sped away from the scene. Pablo drove and they headed towards downtown Manhattan on Second Avenue. Pablo had a rough idea where he was heading but he was not certain. They saw an old homeless man sitting alongside the curb and they stopped to ask him directions.

"Yeh! I know where you want to go, offer me twenty dollars for the directions and you got it," the derelict said.

Pablo stopped the car in front of the shoe store. It was closed and they decided to wait until morning before going inside.

Francis drove listening to the GPS in the car taking him to Monterrey where he had information that the Sinaloa Cartel had built a fortress in the hills. At that moment he had no idea as to how he would approach Emanuel Borgosa but as his adrenaline poured into his body, he kept alert, his mind racing with a variety of scenarios. The package of cocaine laden with the Anthrax bacteria was on the passenger's side of the car, and his suit and jar of the special latex cream were in the trunk.

It was 8:30 in the morning and both Emanuel and Pablo had fallen asleep waiting in the car for someone to open the shoe store. Pablo woke first and saw two men walking into the sore, both dressed well in tailored suits carrying briefcases in their hands.

"Hey ass-hole wake up it time to rock and roll." Pablo said shaking the sleeping Emanuel awake.

Both boys got out of the car and Emanuel stuck the gun further down inside his waist. They walked into the store but did not see the two men who had just walked in before them.

"Hey, is anyone here?" Pablo called out.

A door in the rear of the store opened and one of the men walked out towards them slowly.

"What do you boys want?" he asked.

"We just spoke to Danny and he said since I was his runner for the last few years that maybe we could become sellers of the product," Emanuel said gripping his hand tighter and tighter on the gun.

"You kids must be kidding you are too young to sell shoes."

"We did not come here to learn how to sell shoes," Emanuel continued."

As he spoke the second man came out and asked, "What the fuck do these kids want here?"

"We want to become sellers of the product Danny had me deliver for him for the last few years. We have a better market than he could have ever developed. For God's sake we got the whole High School and many friends who would buy from us being that we are so close to them, and I do not mean selling them shoes."

"Why don't you kids just take off, I don't know what you are talking about. Get lost"

As the second man said this, Emanuel withdrew the gun from his belt and shot the man in the chest. He rapidly turned the gun on the other man to stop him from any retaliation.

"Your friend Danny is now laying on a sidewalk uptown slowly bleeding to death. If you guys want the same I will be happy to accommodate you," Emanuel said moving closer to the man.

Pablo came over and patted the man down finding a loaded pistol in his jacket holster.

"Now I don't know if others are coming here, but if you cannot send us on the path we request, they will find two dead guys here on the floor."

From the floor the man who was shot breathed heavily and said, "Take them in the back and give them the information and damn it get me to a hospital."

Pablo asked," Is there any-one else coming here?"

The man said "no, it is just the two of us who are here to package certain goods."

"You mean package drugs, correct?" Emanuel said.

"Yes, you get it. What do we do with him?" He said pointing to the bleeding man on the floor.

"Is there a dumpster in the back alley of this store?" Pablo asked. "Yes."

"Good," Emanuel said shooting the man on the floor in the face.

"Now let's get him out of here dump him in the trash, and then you can give us the information we will want."

Francis stopped the car and put on his protective suit and rubbed the exposed parts of his body with the cream. Slowly he walked towards the wrought iron fence and rang the bell placed on the brick wall adjacent to the gate.

It took Emanuel, now called Manny ten years to rise up in the organization and become a leader at the tender age of twenty six. He and Pablo, who was always by his side managed to develop a large trade and they were both promoted to the status of lieutenants in the Cartel. During this time Manny went to Harvard, produced clients there, and when he entered the business world as an investment banker, he worked for the Cartel organizing hidden and quiet cells all over the United States. Alonso de Hojeda, the present head of the Cartel met many times with Manny and had Manny as his guest in the Monterrey compound often. Alonso was proud of Manny and envisioned him as the next successor to the throne of the Sinaloa Cartel. Alonso was now eighty years old and was tired of the work involved in keeping the Cartel controlled, fighting off the Mexican authorities and the U.S. drug agents

Manny took control immediately and realized that providing the U.S. with methamphetamine would be easier, less detectable, easier to produce than either cocaine or heroin. He still kept growing the marijuana, however, with some portions of the U.S. in the processing the legalization of medical or public consumption of marijuana the market would decrease. Drug detecting dogs had not as yet become trained to detect "meth", and it could be imported into the states in solid, liquid, or gaseous form. It was fast becoming the favorite drug of the younger population, and Manny's actuary studies demonstrated a potential population of at least one million users in the states. He began sending it to the states in soda cans, musical instruments, cheeses, and almost any form of carrying methodology the imagination could generate.

Francis stood on the veranda steps in front of the opening door at the home of Emanuel Borgosa. A young woman, perhaps in her twenties stood before him. She was blonde, quite trim, and wore a flowing gown which rustled in the breeze. She wore little makeup and smiled a generous smile revealing a perfect set of white teeth that glistened. She waved a welcome hand and asked Francis to enter the hallway which was replete with art and statuary, most likely purchased or created by masters in the arts. The floor was covered with bright red plush carpeting and the walls were papered with unique modern designs having depth giving the impression of dimension. Francis thought he was in a theater showing a three dimensional movie.

"Please come in sir," the white teeth in the brilliant skin covered lips that shone as the woman smiled moved with the salutation.

"No doubt you have had a long tiring journey, and sadly I must tell you that Mr. Borgosa was suddenly called in an emergency to New York City."

"Do you know how long he will be away?" Francis asked.

"I have no idea however he left word to make you comfortable until he returns."

Francis pulse raced as he realized that his plan to make a rapid introduction, leave the tainted brick of cocaine, get Emanuel to inhale it, and leave for his home in Miami, Mission accomplished.

"May I ask if you know where he is in the city? I have a much accelerated set of plans with many meetings already scheduled that unfortunately cannot be changed or delayed. I have my own plane and I could be in New York in a matter of hours to meet with Mr. Borgosa at a place of mutual convenience. Can you contact him for me?"

"Your expression of urgency is impressive let me get his personal assistant Mr. Pablo Estevan who might be able to help you more than I can."

"Please have a drink and make yourself comfortable. He should be here in a little while."

Saying this, the woman disappeared behind two white linen covered French doors. Francis sat down and poured himself a half glass of vodka to calm his nerves. He desperately wanted his trek to be over, not delayed, and this sudden change of plans would force him into strange territory, not knowing any more what to expect than he knew when he arrived at the compound in Mexico.

The French doors opened and a burly man, with a full beard, wearing a brightly flowered shirt outside of his pants, with sandals on his feet approached Francis.

"I understand Mr. Domingo that you had an appointment with my boss Mr. Borgosa. I am very sorry that you made this long journey only to have your meeting delayed. Mr. Borgosa was most interested in meeting with you and he offers deeply impassioned apologies. Perhaps you and I can discuss any matters you wanted to discuss with Mr. Borgosa, and we can then come to an agreement if you desire that I can assure you Mr. Borgosa will honor. I am his right hand and have been since we were young. What is on your mind sir?"

"Well Mr. Estevan, my need to speak to Mr. Borgosa is so deeply secret that I could not discuss my interests with anyone else but directly to him. In fact, it is so important that if you can give me an address in New York where I can meet with him, I shall fly directly to Kennedy Airport and arrange for a private limousine to take me to the meeting place."

"I cannot imagine anything being so important and I am told you are a man of great wealth. I shall call Mr. Borgosa and ask his permission for a meeting in New York to take place. Please excuse me. I shall return shortly."

Pablo returned he had a smile on his face. "I have written down for you the address and time that Mr. Borgosa will meet with you. It is a small Italian restaurant In the Bronx, on Archer Avenue called Dominick's. Here the two of you can meet in total secrecy tomorrow evening at 11:00 P.M. as the restaurant is about to close. It is a favorite meeting place for those persons involved with the Italians who deeply respect our efforts, and we theirs. Mr. Borgosa went to meet with them in order to sign an agreement for mutual work."

"Thank you Mr. Estevan, I will now leave. My car is just outside of the gate. Francis all but ran to his car, and left tires screeching.

Chapter 28
Dining

As Virgil Sanderson approached the restaurant Yamal-al-Sham he was impressed by the long line of limousines that were dispensing customers entering the restaurant, he was impressed by the white alabaster columns that looked like typical mid-eastern structures, but had a certain quality of excellence in the skill of the sculptors that created the facing scrolls and the figures that abounded the circumference of the four columns.

In the front of the red carpeted stairs leading to a golden door stood four greeters dressed in clothing akin to pictures of the story book figure Aladdin. Silky turbans wrapped around their heads, flowing multi-colored robes, and toe pointed shoes with small bells extended from the tips. The robes covered blowing pantaloons of very bright yellows, light blue, crimson, and white dyes. It was a scene from a child's story book and yet here it was.

Male customers wore tuxedos, the women gowns, each filed with the adornments of sparkling jewelry. Virgil knew he was out of place and decided not to enter until he could acquire proper clothing.

Roy Schimmel sat at the bar sipping on his beer looking around at the faces of the men both at the bar and sitting at tables. In The Al-Shaiban bar/restaurant the men wore typical Arabic robes some with turbans and most with not. Almost all of the men wore heavy beards with very few clean shaven. The women as was the custom and law had their heads covered with a variety of shawls, some covering the face, most not. Roy was hungry and he asked for a menu. Food plates were listed both in Arabic and in English pounds, not American dollars. Those wearing Sherpa facial coverings were not distinguishable one from the other. The room was clean although the pungent odor of marijuana hung heavy in the air. Far off in one corner of the room three men sat smoking from elaborate pipes blowing the fumes across the room. In his inside jacket pocket Schimmel had a picture of Yussaf Yaddalah and he wondered how he could circulate with it to everyone to ask if they had seen the man or in fact knew him. He knew it was a dangerous task however he felt he had no choice.

He ordered another beer and took the picture out of his pocket and displayed it to the bartender.

"Have you ever seen my comrade here in your restaurant?" Schimmel asked. "We went to college together in England and lost touch with one another. I am here on business and heard he was here in this town and I would like to touch base with him before I leave in a few days."

The bartender shook his head in a definitive no, but suggested that he himself would take the picture to his customers to see if any knew the man in the picture. As the bartender circulated the room, Schimmel watched the reactions on the cafes of those persons looking at the picture. There was no indication of any identification from anyone in the room.

"I am sorry sir no one here can identify your friend."

Schimmel ate his food slowly, some lamb he thought, not his favorite meat. He knew he would have to return to this restaurant again and again throughout the week and he praised the bar tender highly leaving a very large tip.

"The food is delicious, I will return to sample other items on your menu for the next few days that I am here. Perhaps I might get very lucky and either my friend will come in to taste this wonderful food, or perhaps some other customer might recognize his picture."

"You are most gracious sir, and welcome to be here anytime," the bartender said placing the money in a cash drawer under the bar.

Gerald Williamson approached the restaurant Al-Fakeher with caution. He had an ankle 20 millimeter pistol on his right leg, he had on a Velcro bullet proof vest, and he wore his Sanyo wrist radio as did both Sanderson and Schimmel. The restaurant was no more than a small diner located in a darkened alley between two warehouses and had but one small steel door illuminated by a flickering neon sign. He cautiously opened the door and walked into murkiness and semi-darkness. It was difficult to see the whole room because of the dimness and some of the patrons at tables appeared to be only shadows. He was dressed as a tourist wearing an opened white shirt, khaki pants poorly pressed, leather boots that were soiled and scuffed. On his head he wore a woolen cap that was pulled down over his forehead and ears. He had not washed his face or hands and instead rubbed and mud onto his skin. Williamson sat down at a table with his back to a wall and through the dimness and smoke he was able to get some type of panoramic scene of the interior of the diner and its occupants. He knew in a matter of moments someone, curious or looking for money or drugs would approach him and he was ready to respond. At times during his ten deployments to Afghanistan he needed to do things that would clearly upset the liberal minded. There were times he had killed, not only armed soldiers of the enemy, but doubtful persons who he felt threatened his safety and that of his men. He hated the Arabs deeply and knew he would not hesitate to use deadly force if necessary at any time to anyone. In fact he was very surprised to pass the Psychological screenings conducted at Shalom Village prior to him being selected to be on the team. As a teenager he was inconstant trouble with both his school and his parents. He did not have any love for either and it made him happy to be a bully, never regretting his actions but deriving pleasure from them.

He was bright and consoled himself that he was suffering from PTSD, but able to hide the anxiety and depression so often associated with the condition. He had seen many dead bodies both enemies and friends. He had seen the result of beheading with bodies headless planted alongside roads by ISIS in Iraq. He was ready to die, but he was not ready to give up without a struggle. Here he was in the filthy pit of his enemy ready to do anything to find out information about the terrorist Yussaf Yaddalah.

Williamson motioned to the waitress to come to his table. He showed her the picture and saw immediately recognition on her face.

"I am sorry sir, but I do not know this man."

"Do not lie to me lady, I can see it in your face, you know him and I want you to show me who else in this stink hole knows him as well."

"I have no knowledge of this man, you mistake my behavior."

"Bullshit, I need to know who he is and where I can find him. Now point out who here can tell me that."

The waitress was scared and she rotated her body and with a tiny motion of her hand she pointed to two men sitting at the bar.

"Now that is more like it, now go do your waiting and do not go over to those two men or else you might get hurt. Understand?"

Without saying another word, she went behind a pair of swinging doors most likely into the kitchen.

"Williamson got up from his table and walked over to the bar and stood behind the two men the waitress had pointed out. He took out the picture of Yussaf Yaddalah and placed it onto the bar in front of the men. At the same time he withdrew a six inch serrated hunting knife from his belt and placed it against the neck of one of the men.

"Who is he and where do I find him. Any bullshit and this guy will be breathing in his own blood?"

The man sitting to Williamson's left grabbed the picture and quickly crumpled it and threw it on the floor. Within a fraction of a second Williamson thrust the knife through the man's hand pinning him to the top of the counter.

"I will not take any shit from anyone, you, come with me," Williamson said to the other man acting before the crowd could respond to the first man's scream. "Move your ass now." He grabbed the man by the nape of his neck and his shoulders dragging him onto his feet. At the same time he reached down withdrew his gun and fired two shots into the ceiling.

"Anyone moves and you go to meet Allah in a hurry," Williamson said leaving the diner pulling the man along into the dark alley.

Pushing the man against the brick wall and holding the gun to his forehead, he asked, "Who is he and where do I find him?"

"He is the great warrior Yussaf, he is a hero, and he stays in Sana'a, never coming into the city. He will kill me if he finds out I have told you anything."

"Guess what, I am going to save him the trouble, and saying this Williamson shot the man in the head killing him instantly. Because the silencer was on his gun, the shot was not heard. Williamson walked quietly to a dark street corner and activated his watch/ phone. He called Sanderson and Schimmel and told them that Yussaf Yaddalah was in Golden Bar Tourist hotel. They were to meet outside the hotel in two hours. Williamson and his two comrades stood in front of the entrance to the hotel.

"How the hell did you find out where he was?" Schimmel asked.

"Oh I needed to persuade a customer in the diner I was in. It did not take much effort before he told me of this place."

"Do you have plan, I mean we need to take him alive and bring him back to the village," Sanderson said lighting a cigarette.

"I think you two should just go in and sit down on some chairs if they have a lobby. I will go to the desk and try to find out what room Yaddalah is in. If I do I will either go to the stairs or the elevator if they have one. You two follow me," Williamson said, walking through the hotel door and walking over to the aged and decrepit desk behind which was an old woman. Sanderson and Schimmel sat down in two torn arm chairs waiting to see if Williamson was successful

Williamson walked over to the woman and asked for the number of the room of Yussaf Yaddalah.

"We don't give out room numbers to strangers, especially to strangers, the old woman responded.

"No ma'am, you do not understand, I am Mr. Yaddalah's physician and he called me saying he had some type of stomach virus. Here in my pocket I have medication for him. If I do not get to him rapidly, he will be very mad, and I am certain you know what happens when he is angry," Williamson said placing his hand in his jacket pocket in which he had a pistol. In this pocket he also had a vial of breath sweetener's which he quickly showed to the woman.

"This is the medication he needs, now please tell me his room number so I can make him feel better."

"Room 407, you can take the elevator, she said."

"Does he live alone?" Williamson asked.

"No he has two men with him and one woman," she continued.

"If he is contagious, is there an empty room next to 407 where I can treat him without infecting the others?"

"Yes 405 two doors down is now empty."

Williamson walked to the elevator and Schimmel and Sanderson got up from their chairs and followed him. They entered room 405 and discussed a plan.

"I am going out on the ledge and go through the window shooting. You two will crash through the door at my signal on your watch. We need to coordinate and be certain not to shoot one another. We kill the two aids, and the girl. Be certain the silencers are on. Whoever is closest to Yadallah grab him and we go back to room 405. Let's signal Henry at the village to have a plane ready for us at Sanaa Airport. He most likely will send one in from Riyadh Saudi Arabia where there is a strong American presence. We will keep Yadallah in the room until one of us can abduct a vehicle down on the street. We get in and drive to the Airport. How does that sound?" Williamson asked.

"Fine" both men responded.

Williamson opened a window and crawled out onto the thin ledge protruding from the ancient brick structure. A strong wind was blowing and he almost lost his footing. To look down the four stories of the ancient building would be to incite vertigo. He came to the window of room 407 and very cautiously looked in. Two men were smoking cigars watching a soccer game on the television. The woman was opening a refrigerator. Yadallah was not visible in the room.

However, he had to be there. In the room he could see there was one bedroom and a bathroom as well as the small kitchen living room area.

Williamson texted his men who were now outside the door in the hallway in front of room 407. The signal glowed in red text. NOW! NOW! NOW.

Williamson crashed through the window shooting and hitting the two men. Schimmel shot the woman in the head killing her instantly. A man, Yussaf Yaddalah came out of the bathroom gun in hand and he was instantly tackled by Sanderson who wrestled him to the ground; disarming him and grabbing his hands behind his back to wrap strong plastic ties around his wrists.

"Let's get the fuck out of here and back to 405." Williamson screamed. At the same time Sanderson took the elevator to the street and walked slowly through the lobby. Once on the street he broke the driver's side window of a car and hot- wired it to start. He immediately texted Williamson that he was in the car. The red one about four cars to the left of the street entryway.

Schimmel took the elevator down and walked to the car. Williamson slowly walked Yaddalah past the female clerk and said, "He needs to go to the hospital."

The woman did not look up and Williamson took Yaddalah through the small lobby out onto the street and pushed him into the back seat of the car. Sanderson drove slowly knowing it would take about one half hour to get to the airport, board the plane and be on the way to Poland.

Chapter 29
Face to Face

Francis drove just under the speed limit to get to the airport and his waiting plane. Not being able to confront Emanuel Borgosa was a tremendous disappointment for him. He ran onto the plane and gave the pilot instructions to take him to LaGuardia Airport in New York. He called to have his car waiting for him upon arrival. Once he was settled he went into the planes bathroom and washed the cream off his face and hands as well as taking off the protective suit. He knew he would redo the application of the ream and don the suit when he landed, but the suit was uncomfortable and too warm.

He sat back in his seat and took a long deep swallow of the iced bourbon in the glass. Francis dialed the coded number for Henry Calico in Poland.

"Henry this is Francis, I am on my way to New York. Borgosa was not in Mexico as I believed thus I am flying to New York to meet with him in a restaurant in the Bronx."

"Francis I cannot begin to tell you of the horrendous mess the bombing at the village created. We found Myron's body and gave him a Jewish ceremonial burial here. I guess millions of his faith met their deaths under the unforgiveable actions of the Nazis. Three of my group went into Yemen to find the perpetrator of this horror, and I just got a text from one of them that they successfully captured the maniac and that they were on a plane headed to Poland, and to us. Charles has been very depressed since we landed here and saw what had occurred. I wish he would seek help but he refuses to face his depression. I think he has never been emotionally stable under stress since the death of his brother. I think once the three of us are together again we can convince him to seek professional help. We will have to go to the U.S. Embassy and turn over the perpetrator for questioning and finality. I understand from one of my men that acquiring Yaddalah involved some shooting, and we can get the details once they have returned. I wish you luck. Have you been successful in your previous hunts?"

"Well yes and no. I am certain of one and not certain of the other, but it is what it is. My third acquisition will, believe me not be a disappointment to me."

"Come back soon. I need to see your smiling face, and we both need to help Charles. Construction here has begun again, and is under a full head of steam. Have success and be well. Perhaps we all can return to our original tasks, and return to the club."

Francis disconnected and let himself fall into a deep sleep. He was physically and emotionally exhausted, and the most important portion of his quest lay ahead of him in a New York restaurant.

Dominic's restaurant was a very small dinning place with only ten tables in the front section of the area. Behind the kitchen was another much larger room in which members of the Mafia of New York met for business meetings. Manny Borgosa was speaking from the "head seat" of the rectangular table. Sitting to his right was Alfredo Alvarez, a former National Football League wide receiver. He was wearing a silk suit and necktie around his enormous wide neck. His shirt sleeves ended with gold cufflinks. In front of him on the table was a notebook with what appeared to be legers. Next to him sat Tony Obbligato an old country gangster with warrants out for his arrest in three states and a search for him has been conducted by Interpol for years. Somehow with the assistance of many Mafia brothers he escaped all attempts to capture him. He was a professional assassin and was responsible for at least the deaths of eighteen persons, many of whom were considered data leakers by the mob. Tony in his years, all eighty of them had become quite proficient in computer technology, and he was the keeper of the influx of illegal cash brought to the New York Bank of Western Children, a privately owned bank created by the Mafia in which the cash was stored in a massive underground vault.

Francis entered the restaurant and was greeted by an aged woman who stood behind a counter on which a cash register prominently rose from its resting place on a grape colored velour counter top.

It was six P.M. and people were drifting into the small restaurant the old woman motioned to Francis to sit at a table already occupied by a young couple, most likely in attendance across the street at Einstein Medical College. Dominic's restaurant maintained a kitchen that was tended to by three woman wives of some of the Mafia bosses in New York, who prepared all the food ordered by customers. No menu was on the tables with prices attached. The menu listed a large variety of Italian favorites, and all orders from patrons were cooked in the kitchen freshly prepared. The wine list was extensive and no prices were listed.

"Ma'am, I am here to speak to Mr. Borgosa. Can you direct me to him. I am told he is in this establishment. He is expecting me. The woman pointed to the closed curtain and told Francis to wait until he was summoned.

Francis opened the curtain and sat on a bench alongside the heavy door. A massive man, holding an automatic weapon stood on the opposite side of the bench watching Francis with piercing eyes.

"Are you here to see Mr. Borgosa?" he asked.

Not wanting to create any suspicion, Francis took out a cigarette and asked the grotesque man if he had a light. The man reached into a pocket of his khaki jacket and produced a lighter and reached over to light Francis' cigarette.

"Never saw you before," Mr. Monster said in a deep baritone voice that was raspy and seemed full of mucous.

"Never been here before, but I have some business to discuss with Mr. Borgosa, will he be long?"

"Never know, he is in a monthly meeting with some of his boys, and all's I do is to stand here to provide protection for anyone in the room. Not that they cannot protect themselves, but the New York cops and FBI agents can show up here at any time and I am to delay them by any means possible to give anyone in the conference room time to clean themselves. There are special portals in which they can dispose of weapons or samples immediately. In my hand I hold a warning device that will turn the overhead lights off and on. We would not use a signal that created any noise."

"Sounds impressive," Francis said breaking out into a sweat hoping that the moisture would not lessen the effectiveness of the protective cream he had carefully spread on his face and scalp.

"Tony lets go over the monthly figures," Manny asked.

"Well let me look. These are the figures from the forty states that we control, and I really think we are improving our take."

Tony read:

1. Prostitution — $12,000,000.00
2. Marijuana — $1,000,425.00 (we are being hurt by the legalization. People from all over the country are going to those states that have legalized to buy.)
3. Cocaine — $25,000,000.00
4. Meth — $16,000,000.00
5. Heroin — $31,000,000.00
6. Ecstasy — $9,000,000.00
7. Oxycodone — $5,000,000.00

8. Synthetics $500,000.00 (our cost in getting these over the counter drugs from the Chinese is very high. They want the market for themselves and are selling directly by order from retail stores.)

"Are we on target Tony?" Manny asked.

"Yeh! Boss, but we need to get more very high quality coke for the elite. They want it, and can easily pay for it. These high class junkies are in a separate class. There kids who get large allowances can pay especially for Ecstasy and for Coke. We know they ultimately go up the ladder looking for greater highs, but that takes time. Our greatest buyers in the kid's league are those in the middle schools. I think that soon the upper aged kids in the elementary schools will join them."

Francis heard a clicking sound alongside him and the door slowly opened.

"Mr. Frankenstein said, "You can go in now."

Francis waked casually into the room and sat down in the seat to the left of Manny Borgosa. They shook hands and Manny introduced Francis to the other two men. Francis clutched his brick of tainted cocaine tightly in his lap as Manny described that Francis was here to investigate a deal which would bring the purest cocaine to the mob for distribution to those of varying degrees of multimillions of dollars.

Francis placed the brick on the table top and cut into the top of the seal.

"Would you gentleman like to take a sample?" he asked.

Manny took the brick of tainted cocaine in front of him and using a curved tool he spread out four lines of it on the table. He gave each person including Francis a brightly colored straw. "For sanitary purposes," he said inhaling the line of cocaine in front of him. Alfredo, Tony and finally Francis each took their turn. Alfredo's face turned a brilliant red and he leaned his head back looking up to the ceiling.

"Holy shit!" he said rocking his body left and right.

"Mr. Domingo this is the best stuff I have ever experienced. Clearly we can do business. Give me your address and I will have papers prepared for our deal."

"No, I move around a lot Mr. Borgosa," Francis replied, not wanting the mob to be able to track his whereabouts after the three men contracted the anthrax and died.

"It will be better if I call you in a few days, and E-mail you my conception of a deal Mr. Borgosa. If you find the terms satisfactory we can begin to do business together. I shall be in touch with you. Have a nice day. I will be happy to leave the brick here for any further use you may have of it. Thank you."

Chapter 30
Boom

The Cessna glided through the smooth air almost silently. Prior to leaving Yemen Yaddalah asked if he could change from his robes into more Western attire. Williamson followed him into his room where Yaddalah put on a pair of jeans, placed his belt into the waist loops, clipped the ends of the suspenders, and took off his slippers putting on a pair of loafers. Williamson placed handcuffs on Yaddalah's wrists with Yaddalah's hands around his back.

Once on the plane Sanderson sat next to Yaddalah. Williamson sat in front of him and Schimmel sat in back of him. They had been traveling for hours and the plane was off the coast of Rumania over the darkness of the Black Sea. Williamson was asleep and snoring loudly. Schimmel was reading a book, and Sanderson stared blankly out of the window.

"I have to go to the bathroom," Yaddalah asked Sanderson.

"Alright, but I go with you," Sanderson replied getting up from his seat.

"Could you remove these handcuffs so I can tend to myself?" Yaddalah asked.

"Well I guess you can't go out of the window, because there is no window in there. Alright, I will take the cuffs off and I will be right outside the door," Sanderson said removing the handcuffs.

Yaddalah went into the bathroom and immediately looked for a source of electric current that lit the lights. He stood on the top of the toilet and reached up to the ceiling pulling the lights casing off as silently as he could. Behind the light source was electrical wiring. Yaddalah pulled at the wires and with his teeth he removed the plastic coating that acted as a deterrent against any sparking.

Once the wires were removed he took the positive and negative wires pressing them into the fabric of his suspenders causing a massive explosion. When he changed his clothing he donned the C4 belt, suspenders and shoes he had made with the 3-D copier. Persons in Rumania saw the explosion over the ocean and paid little attention to it. Since no flight plan had been entered in Yemen and no intelligence had been acquired about the covert mission, no one had reason to search for the plane or any survivors of the blast. There were none.

Henry and Charles began to worry when the plane was hours late. Checks upon weather conditions on the planes route revealed perfect flying weather. They wondered why the plane was late, and no reports came into their network from any of the three men except for the initial report that Yaddalah had been apprehended and they were on their way back to Poland. Two days passed and still no word. Charles searched the web and found reports of a strange explosion that it up the sky in an area over the Black Sea. He had an naval tracking station search for evidence of the explosion and found out that it had occurred directly in the flight path of the Cessna and the time it occurred was accurate as to where the plane should have been. Both Charles and Henry understood that somehow the plane exploded and was lost with their volunteers and Yaddalah. Both wondered if this was retribution for the evil Yaddalah had brought to the village. No, to his insane people he was now most likely a hero, a god, in heaven with Allah. Charles felt completely let down and his depression worsened. The loss of the three men was almost more than he could bear. The carnage at the village, the loss of the man responsible for it, and the loss of his dear friends Myron and Donald were conditions that he could not process.

Henry seeing his friend in the deepening depressive state suggested that they return to the United States. He told Charles that he might be needed to complete his school protection program, and that he, Henry needed to make certain that the hospital and clinics were clear of corrupted medications. He would contact Francis. And all three would meet at the usual time and date back at the club. Henry had no idea of what had occurred with Francis, and he prayed that no harm had come to him.

Chapter 31
The Golf Club

Francis was the first to arrive at the club. He read in the New York Times about the three persons dead from Anthrax who had all eaten at the Bronx restaurant Dominic's. He was aware of the fact that Emanuel Borgosa was one of them along with his henchmen Alfredo and Tony. He did not know who the other three persons were who became ill and he felt badly about any additional illnesses. Apparently some of the Anthrax spores were in the air and a small amount was inhaled by customers in the restaurant. The Mayor of New York had called in the CDC to be certain that no Anthrax bacteria threatened any other area however the CDC reported that it was in the cocaine and no deadly amount of Anthrax spores were in the air. The restaurant was closed. There was no report of any large sums of money in a vault were reported in the article. Thus except for the death of all three cartel villains Francis felt satisfied that he did his best to avenge Donald and to rid the world of three vicious unconscionable harmful criminals. He knew others would quickly step into the leadership roles that he had created openings in. He accomplished what his revengeful needs were.

Charles went directly to Boston before joining Henry and Francis. He thought long and hard about what other measures he could put into action to protect the children of the Boston schools. On his trip back to Boston he viewed a video about rescue dogs. They were trained to help the blind. They could sniff out drugs, and some could sniff out cancer of certain types in humans. These remarkable dogs responded to all sorts of commands including sensing if their owners were about to have a stroke. He thought. Why not place a rescue trained dog in each school to sniff out weapons on students, to sniff out drugs, and to react to potential violence. He immediately asked the Society of Humane Rescue to purchase hundreds of dogs, train them and place one dog in each targeted school. Once he was assured this would be done he boarded his plane and headed to the golf club.

Dr. Henry Calico diverted from the meeting to speak to Dr. Bob Waters and receive assurances that all medications in the facilities were proven safe. He wrote an E-mail message to Chi Kahn the medical director of the Beijing Laboratory warning him of any tampering with medications that went to his hospital and clinics. He did not trust the Chinese who he felt might attempt to pollute other manufacturer's medications. He told Chi Kahn that all United States facilities were to be careful ordering medical product, and he assured him that the United States FDA and CDC would constantly assess the quality to medications purchased abroad. He knew he could not contain or reduce, or stop on line purchases made by the public once they obtained prescriptions from their own personnel physicians. He spent a great deal of money having public awareness advertising play on major television channels warning the United States citizens to be extremely careful about medications purchased that did not have FDA approvals. Large government institutions such as the veteran's administration and certain Medicare advantage plans, as well as Medicaid providers he felt would not be as conscientious given that their line of profitability was so small that they would take risks and purchase medications even those still produced in China. Charles had unwavering faith in Dr. Waters, and he glowed when he saw lines of residents being treated in his facilities.

Both Henry and Charles agreed to allow Johnny Falcone continue to construct Shalom Village. Enormous security measures were in place and to both men the confidence they felt was unmeasurable. Henry remained concerned about the depression Charles was in and he hoped against hope that when Charles saw the achievements that Charles had created in the Boston schools, he would slowly emerge from his depressive state. Henry had prescribed some Buspar for Charles which seemed to help Charles regain his individuality and lighten his personality.

"Well here we are, no longer a foursome with an extra to play. But here we are with our mission accomplished to this point, "Francis said to his remaining two allies."

"Yes, we will miss our buddies dearly. They were our companions, and both felt that the mission Myron sent us out on was for good."

"I agree Henry added. Myron's mission was for us to each create something of monumental value for the good of mankind, and in our own way we achieved our goals."

"I think we need to find at least one other golfer, a man or woman who would be committed to our concepts and be able to carry out another set of missions next year, "Charles added.

The three golfers took their golf bags to their respective golf carts. In a hurry to get to the first tee, Francis collided with another golf cart in which a woman was driving.

"You damn asshole, who do you think you are?" she screamed at him.

"For God's sake lady, don't have a fit. I can easily repair or replace your cart. Whatever the cost, no matter," Francis said.

"I do not need you to pay for me," the woman responded. I am eminently wealthy and can pay by myself."

"Charles came over to the fracas and quieted everything down.

"How is your golf game?" he asked the woman.

"Good enough to play with you I am sure, "she responded with disdain in her voice.

"Why then won't you play with me and my three friends?"

As they drove off Charles asked the woman how she felt about certain abuses that were occurring in the country; drugs, crime, politics etc. Her responses about all the charities she funded drew Charles attention and before the game was over he asked her plainly on the eighteenth hole if she would like to join the group.

"Only if I can be in charge of all decisions" she answered.

THE END

www.ingramcontent.com/pod-product-compliance
Lightning Source LLC
Chambersburg PA
CBHW060303290526
45789CB00001B/393